# THE HIMALAYAN DISTRICTS OF KOOLOO, LAHOUL, AND SPITI

# THE HIMALAYAN DISTRICTS OF KOOLOO, LAHOUL, AND SPITI

By

CAPT. A.F.P. HARCOURT, BENGAL STAFF CORPS

GYAN

*Published by*

Gyan Publishing House
5, Ansari Road
Daryaganj, New Delhi-110002
Phone: 011-47034999, 9811692060
E-mail: books@gyanbooks.com

*Distribution Network*
gyanbooks.com
India, USA, Canada, UK, Australia, France



ISBN : 978-81-212-9810-0 (PB)
First Published, 1871

2nd Impression 2023

*Printed at:* Gyan Press, Delhi.



**THE HIMALAYAN DISTRICTS OF KOOLOO, LAHOUL, AND SPITI**
Author: Capt. A.F.P. HARCOURT

THE

# HIMALAYAN DISTRICTS

OF

# KOOLOO, LAHOUL, AND SPITI.

BY

CAPT. A. F. P. HARCOURT, BENGAL STAFF CORPS,

Assistant Commissioner, Punjab.

"A good land, a land of brooks of water, of fountains and depths that spring out of valleys and hills; a land of wheat, and barley, and vines, and fig-trees, and pomegranates; a land of oil, olive, and honey; a land wherein thou shalt eat bread without scarceness, thou shalt not lack anything in it; a land whose stones are iron, and out of whose hills thou mayest dig brass."

*WITH ILLUSTRATIONS BY THE AUTHOR.*

# CONTENTS.

## CHAPTER IX.



## CHAPTER X.



## CHAPTER XI.



## CHAPTER XII.

# APPENDIX.

# LIST OF PLATES.

# THE HIMALAYAN DISTRICTS

OF

# KOOLOO, LAHOUL, AND SPITI.

## CHAPTER I.

### INTRODUCTORY REMARKS.

IN September, 1869, I addressed Mr. Thornton, Secretary to the Punjab Government, as to the advisability of my furnishing a Report on Kooloo, and in reply I was informed, that a "full report on Kooloo would be thankfully received, and probably printed at Government expense;" and Colonel Coxe, the Commissioner of the Division, in his letter of 8th October, 1869, to address of the Deputy Commissioner of Kangra, suggested that I should throw, what he was good enough to consider, the "interesting matter" contained in my diaries as

Assistant-Commissioner of Kooloo, into the form of a report, that "might be submitted officially to Government." I have, therefore, during the last year of my term of office in Kooloo, been diligently engaged in collecting facts of more general interest regarding the people and country, which have been so immediately under my care for now nearly two years. It was at first my intention to merely collate such information as I could acquire into the form of a report; but I found the work grew in my hands, and I became convinced that no mere report could do justice to the subject matter, which daily increased in volume. It may be, and probably will be, urged that there surely cannot be much to tell of a country like Kooloo, known to few, and occupying such a very insignificant place in the geography or history of India; but it is to be recollected, that within the subdivision is comprised an area of over 6,000 square miles; that the district now known as Kooloo was once the territory of an independent line of sovereigns, some eighty of whom sat on the throne, many of them holding sway over every ruler in their vicinity; that three distinct races, at least, reside in its present limits; that the climate, scenery, the country, and the people are unlike what are to be found anywhere else in India; and, finally, that this large extent of British dominion has not to this day, I believe, been ever reported on in its entirety by any one of the officers who have had charge of the subdivision. I am fully aware that, while I may consider Kooloo a very interesting land, and that no pains can be too great in eliciting everything concerning it, there may be not a few who will fail to see the necessity of entering so fully into what they may deem to be, comparatively speaking, petty details; but whether or not my time has been wasted in compiling these papers, I must leave to my readers to decide.

I have endeavoured to make this account of Kooloo as succinct as possible; and I have purposely desisted from writing more amply on the history of the country, and various other points that might, perhaps, have been legitimately dilated upon; but it was necessary to draw the line somewhere, and I have been obliged to content myself with what, after all, is but a bare outline of the more important, or more interesting, matters that have come under my observation.

It was, at one time, my desire to have first written the history of Kooloo, the rough notes of which I have for a long time had by me; but there were difficulties regarding dates, which I have not yet been able to clear up; and as I had not time this year * to do both the History and the General Account of the subdivision, I have elected to postpone the former till a more fitting opportunity may occur.

Much might have been added to the chapters on religions, languages, &c., and an account of the legendary tales and peculiar customs existing in parts of the district would alone almost make up a respectable

* This was written in 1870.

volume; but often, when on the point of entering more fully on these particulars, I have held my hand, fearing that my readers' patience might, perhaps, have been already too unduly taxed. Doubtless it will be remarked that there is hardly any notice taken in these pages of the Central Asian trade, but this omission has been intentional. I could have told but little that the public are not aware of already, and, although the commerce that finds a passage between the Punjab and East Turkestan certainly takes the route *viâ* Kooloo, yet the subject can hardly be deemed a local one, and its due consideration will always remain more fittingly with the officer deputed as British agent to Ladakh. But my main reason for keeping silence on the trade question is that this subject is not one that can be dismissed in a few paragraphs, nor can it be deemed altogether germane to a report, intended more particularly to set forth the social customs and manners of the people in this subdivision.

I have, in fact, had to make selection as to the points on which I could write with the clearest knowledge; and, in choosing those that I believed to be of greater general interest, I have necessarily had to leave out much that might, with propriety, have been treated upon.

It is with extreme regret that I shall resign, on my approaching departure for England, the charge of Kooloo, a tract of country which, taking it all in all, is not, I believe, equalled out of Europe; but I shall not have been there nor shall I have written in vain, if these papers may haply serve to draw fuller attention to its matchless scenery and fine climate, which have not, as yet, been nearly so fully appreciated as they deserve to be. My acknowledgments to the various gentlemen to whom I am indebted for information have been recorded, I believe, in each instance, and I can only again repeat here my thanks for the assistance I have derived from their works.

## CHAPTER II.

Situation of Kooloo, its subdivisions.—Area of Kooloo and of each of its subdivisions, with cultivated area, revenue, and population.—General Geographical Features, showing boundaries, mountains, valleys, and rivers.

THE outlying district of Kooloo, comprising the minor subdivisions of Kooloo proper, or the Upper Beas valley, Wuzeeri-Rupi, Seoraj, Lahoul, and Spiti, forms a portion of the Deputy-Commissionership of Kangra, than which, however, it is nearly three times as large, and from which it is distant some eighty miles. Considering this tract of country as one compact whole, it may be said to lie between 31° 20′ and 32° 55′ lat. and 76° 50′ and 78° 35′ lon.; being bounded on the north by Ladakh, on the east by Chinese Tartary, on the south by Bussahir and the small states of Kotghur, Komharsen, and Shangri, the river Sutledj being the dividing line; Sookhaet, Mundee, Bara Bunghal (an almost inaccessible offshoot of the Kangra district), and Chumba following each other in succession up its western side.

The total area of Kooloo is 6,025 square miles, and the tables annexed will serve to show how this area is distributed, with the revenue derivable from the subdivision, and such other statistics as may properly be here recorded; * the whole country being divided off into what in local parlance are termed "kothees," which vary in size and in the amount of revenue they respectively pay in to the State.

In the Upper Beas valley there are seventeen "kothees," in Wuzeeri-Rupi six, in Seoraj twenty-five, in Lahoul fourteen, and in Spiti five; each of which has its own headman with assistants, whose separate powers and functions will be treated on hereafter.

---

* *Vide* Appendix.

A glance at the map will at once portray how completely on the north, north-west, east, and south-east, the entire district here referred to is enclosed by mountains.

Commencing with Lahoul, we find that to the west a lofty range separates that country from Chumba, there being but one break, through which flows the Chundra Bagha; the mountains sweeping round to the south-east constituting the boundary-line between Kooloo and Lahoul, and in an irregular line trending down still to the south-east, where they flank the southern shore of the river Chundra. Reverting again to the northern frontier, we find the Bara Lacha range, which to the north stretches in gentle slopes to the rivers Ling-ti and Tserap, and then in a series of lofty peaks, falls away to the south, skirting the left bank of the river Chundra, and sending its spurs to meet those that splay off from the direction of the Rohtung Pass.

The line of mountains that hem in Spiti to the north, and separate it from Ladakh, is a continuation of the Bara Lacha range, that in rude angles pierces upwards to the north, and then falls again to the south-east, and, under the name of the Parung range, leads towards the Sutledj. This river, however, never impinges on Spiti, the southern boundary of which is the huge Manirung chain, that divides it from Bussahir. Between these two ranges flows the Spiti river. Running up between Spiti on one side, and Seoraj, Wuzeeri-Rupi, and Kooloo on the other, rises a line of heights, which, commencing at the south-westernmost point in Spiti, bears to the north-west till the Rohtung range is touched, just above the village of Juggutsookh, in the Upper Beas valley.

Commencing from the snowy peak M (20,356 feet), which may be considered nearly the most northern point of this portion of the subdivision, the Rohtung chain penetrates upwards for two miles, and then to the south-west for four more; and as it passes onward to the north-east, to form the boundary-line between Bara Bunghal and

Lahoul, it throws off a line of mountains that, with many lofty peaks, run south by east, dividing Bara Bunghal, Chota Bunghal, and Mundee from Kooloo proper; becoming much reduced in size, as regards their altitude, as they press further south, till, at peak Madanpur (9,149 feet), they wind off altogether into the Mundee state. From Madanpur, the boundary of Mundee runs due east by Bajoura, on the bank of the Beas, that river forming the territorial limit of Kooloo (Wuzeeri-Rupi), down to Larjee, where it is joined by the Tirthan from the south-east; and along this, and its tributary the Bah, the frontier line running due south, continues till it is cut across by the Jalouri range, twenty-five miles as the crow flies, from the point of contact with the Beas at Bajoura. Mundee, still conterminous with Kooloo, remains so for six miles more to the south, following the course of a branch of the Bisna, which at Baito village flows into Sookhaet territory, and shortly after joins the Sutledj between Fareenoo and Bang.

The boundary-line now runs up the right bank of the Sutledj, that comes down from the north-east, until, after thirty miles, the Kunrad joins the latter from the north, forming the frontier between Kooloo and Bussahir. To the north of this, Spiti runs side by side with Seoraj, the mountains attaining a more imposing height rather to the south-east of the Rohtung range.

Kooloo proper consists of the whole of the north-west part of the country, the limits of which have just been given; the Malauna and Parbuttee streams separating the Upper Beas valley from Wuzeeri-Rupi, that includes the upper portion of the Parbuttee valley, and all to the south of the Parbuttee river and east of the Beas, up to the Larjee torrent, which falls into the Beas at Larjee; Seoraj forming the southern extremity of the subdivision, a species of rough triangle closed in on its southern face by the Sutledj.

The whole of Lahoul may not inaptly

be termed a network of mountains, which intersect it in every direction; and the numerous glaciers, no less than twenty-three in number, form a fair index as to the heights of the ranges that encircle them. On the western side, however, the mountains attain to no great altitude, there being but one peak (Ghasa black cone) over 19,000 feet above the sea-level. In the Bara Lacha range there are many lofty peaks over 18,000 feet in height, and two that are upwards of 20,000 feet. The Rohtung range will be considered as part of Kooloo proper, and I may therefore pass on to notice the mass of mountains that fill up the space between the Bhaga and Chundra rivers. This area is one great ice-bed, broken here and there by lofty heights of impassable rock and snow, that tower to a greater altitude than is elsewhere to be found in Lahoul. At the western shore of the Chundra rises one peak 21,415 feet above the sea-level, to the south of which stretches a vast glacier, twelve miles in length, that is met by another of even greater dimensions; more to the south, the Shigri heights ascend, in several instances, to over 20,000 feet; and following the right bank of the Chundra, we find that river flanked on its northern side by a tier of peaks, the loftiest of which, "Snowy-cone Gaphan," stands 19,212 feet above sea-level.

In Spiti the mountains attain a higher elevation than they do in the sister valley, the Parung range containing one peak, the loftiest in the entire subdivision, marked in the map at 23,064 feet in height, and many in its vicinity are upwards of 20,000 feet above sea-level. It would but weary the reader to refer to every cluster of such peaks; they are to be found interspersed through Spiti; two on its western side are over 21,000 feet in altitude, and the range that bounds it to the south forms but another gigantic barrier that culminates at Manirung snowy peak, 21,646 feet in height. And yet, extraordinary to say, although Spiti is so crowded with chain on chain of tremendous mountains, there is in the whole country but one glacier, and that a small one, lying to the north of the Manirung Pass.

Kooloo is nearly as much shut in by hills as are Lahoul and Spiti. The Rohtung range to the north has one peak (M) 20,356 feet in height; Deotiba, to the east, is 20,417 feet; and the line of watershed between Kooloo and Spiti, to the east, has some very noticeable altitudes, which were referred to more particularly when Spiti was under discussion. On the west, the mountains, after leaving the Rohtung range, gradually diminish in height, leaving the south-west portion of the district comparatively open.

In the interior, the spurs of the encircling mountains splay out into the lower parts of the valley, subsiding into lengthened sweeps of arable land as they approach the Beas; but the eastern portion of Wuzeeri-Rupi is almost to the full as rugged as is Spiti, or Lahoul; and in Seoraj the offshoots of the snowy range stretch, in two distinct though somewhat broken chains, to the western limits of that tract.

The river Chundra rises in the Bara Lacha Pass, in Lahoul, at 16,221 feet above sea-level, and, after a south-easterly course of over thirty miles, turns towards the north-west, being joined by the Bagha at Tandee, eighty miles from its source, the fall up to this point being sixty-five feet per mile. From Tandee, under the name of the Chundra Bagha, it flows on for twelve miles more through Lahoul, passing into Chumba at Jolang, through a break in the range between Chumba and Lahoul, joining the Indus at Mithancote; its "length from source to junction," says Cunningham, "being 950 miles." From a huge bed of snow on the south-eastern slopes of the Bara Lacha Pass, springs the Chundra, which from its commencement is a stream of some size, and quite unfordable a mile from its source. Flowing in a south-easterly direction, it passes through a wild and barren land, where there are no signs of life, the solemn mountains, capped with eternal snow, lying on either side; and thus ushered into existence under such awe-inspiring auspices, it dashes its foaming waters by glacial banks of snow, vast reaches of gravel and decomposed rock, and here stretching into a mighty flood, again subsides into a more stealthy strength, as its icy tide flows onward through a country famed but for sterility and that colossal grandeur that can only be imparted by vast mountains.

No villages adorn its banks, no attempt at cultivation is to be seen, and nothing meets the eye but the never-ending and monotonous cliffs that sweep down in contorted masses to the seething stream, which laps in fierce anger against the banks, and tears them in its wrath as it rushes on. From either side come to it tributaries of a character like its own, and, after a course of thirty miles, it suddenly turns sharply to the west, here being overhung by the glittering Shigri peaks; and now its bed attains its greatest width, and the valley through which the river rolls is on its southern shore moderately level; but still, on the right hand and on the left, rise up the everlasting snows, cresting a disintegrated rock lying below, that ever and anon crumbles from the mass, and crushes with a dull roar into the desert underneath, but to add to the *débris* that is ever crowding over to the river's edge. In several channels the waters flow on till they reach what has been termed the Shigri glacier, though Shigri is the local term for any glacier; and here it is said that, in 1836, the vast accretions of ice bursting forth from the mountains on the left bank of the stream, flung themselves across the river, damming it up for months. The barrier was, however, eventually burst, and the accumulated waters poured onwards, carrying destruction in their rush. Cunningham does not, in his "Ladakh," allude to the cataclysm of the Chundra, and I have not been able to obtain any certain information on this interesting event. There can be little doubt, judging from the quantity of ice collected on the flanks of the mountains that bound the river, that at any day such a disaster may again occur; but no power on earth could avert the catastrophe. The Shigri glacier is, to outward appearance, a mere mass of earth and rock; but, on the side towards the river, it presents a wall of solid ice, and, as its surface is traversed, glittering depths of green ice are occasionally to be met with. In the early morning, when the sun has had little power to melt the ice, the passage of the glacier is comparatively easy, though I doubt whether it would be ever possible to ride over it, for every step has to be conned over, and, as I counted 3,648 of these when I walked over it in August, 1869, it might be safe to put the width of the Shigri at nearly two miles. The glacier is steadily subsiding, and every year is getting lower and lower.

Further down, and on the same bank of the stream, are the remains of another glacier, which, from the accounts of the Spiti people, broke across the Chundra some eighty years ago; and it is an asserted fact that the road into Kooloo by the left bank of the Chundra has more than once had to be given up in consequence of the track being completely obliterated by glaciers.

Now turning to the north-west, the Chundra, shortly after leaving Shigri, passes Koksur, an offshoot of the larger village twelve miles below, two wretched huts, inhabited in the summer only, being the first signs of human life to be met with; a small extent of birch forest growing halfway up the mountain-side to the south. Three miles above the real village of Koksur is a rest-house and out-offices; and now the river enters on a less uninviting country, for in its passage onward the valley widens considerably in several places, and there is a good deal of cultivated ground on the right bank, while on the left there are some few scattered trees, and near the junction with the Bagha, opposite Tandee, these clumps collect together near the village of Muling into a tolerably extensive forest. The greater portion of the entire valley of the Chundra is a desert, in which nothing but grass can grow, and in some of the upper reaches numerous flocks of sheep and goats are annually fed. Some twenty-five miles from its source, the river passes a lake on its left bank, called Chundra-dul, a refreshing sheet of placid green water, about a mile long and as much broad, to the north of which is a plain of fairly good grass. This little oasis, sheltered from the bitter winds, and rejoicing, from its position, in an almost tolerable climate, is a favourite halting-place for shepherds, who bring up large herds from Kangra and Kooloo.

As Gondla is approached, the country opens; and hereabouts is a good deal of cultivation, while the hamlets are larger, and the houses, too, are better built, and are, besides, hemmed in by trees, the pepul and the willow both growing to some size.

On the north side of the valley the mountains take a gentler slope than they do towards Koksur; but on the left bank of the river they rise in almost perpendicular blocks, their peaks, unless where the snow still clings, showing gaunt and spectre-like.

The scenery now becomes very striking, the heights opposite to Gondla ascending to over 20,000 feet in altitude; and between the tremendous hollows in the chasms are masses of snow, which lie piled up heap on heap, from out of which tear cascades that are lost in the gorges underneath. Almost exactly in front of the encamping-ground is one lofty peak, its summit crested with eternal snow, which, in the deeper recesses, has clotted together into an ice-field which impends over the vale, threatening at any moment to sweep over the beetling crags on to the grassy slopes below. Lower down than this, as Cunningham happily puts it, "the bed of the Chundra becomes exceedingly narrow, and the mountains are bare, bleak, and wild, and blasted as if freshly risen from the innermost and fiery depths of the earth," the limestone strata on the left bank being coloured and contorted in the most extraordinary manner.

The Bagha rises on the north-west side of the Bara Lacha Pass, and flowing in a north-westerly direction, joins the Chundra near Tandee, after a course of forty-five miles, with a fall of about 125 feet per mile. A mile from its source, it enters the Suraj-dul, a lake about a mile and a half in circumference, 16,000 feet above sea-level, and escaping through this, flows, for ten or eleven miles, to rather below Zingzingbar, a barren encamping-ground on the road to Leh from Lahoul, and then turning round to the south-west passes Darcha, the last inhabited spot in Lahoul, where it is joined by the Zanskar river (the Kado Tokpo of the map) from the west; and here the Bagha increases in size, and its bed is of great breadth; but it again narrows near Kielung, below which the stream takes a westerly course prior to its junction with the Chundra at Tandee. The lower part of the Bagha valley, towards the villages of Kielung, Kardung, and Baelung, is rich in cultivation, large tracts of level arable land lying between the mountains, and reaching to the river, which, in the latter portion of its course, is confined between steep banks of siliceous rock, through which it pours with great velocity. At Darcha, the most northerly village in the entire subdivision, cultivation becomes more scanty, and beyond this point dies away altogether, while the growth of pencil-cedar, willow, pepul, and kyle,* to be met with below, now ceases entirely, and, to quote from Cunningham, the mountains on the left bank of the Bagha "look barren and hideous, and scathed as with fire, with bare and frightful precipices, so steep that even the snow cannot rest upon them;" but above rise snowy peaks of great beauty, which relieve the landscape, if not from its sterility, at any rate from its drear monotony.

The Lingti river, considered by Cashmere as the boundary between Lahoul and Ladakh, rises considerably to the north-west of the Bara Lacha Pass, and has a south-eastern course till joined by the Yunam, when it turns to the north; the Serchu, which, as

* *Pinus excelsa.*

does the Yunam, springs from the northern slopes of this pass, meeting it a little further on, the combined waters passing the encampment of Lingti (14,213 feet), and falling into the Tserap a few miles to the north. The Tserap rises to the north-west of the Takling-la (pass), in Spiti, and is not, strictly speaking, in our territory; but it receives, on its north-westerly course, several large tributaries; and after its junction with the Lingti, turns to the north, and passes away into Ladakh.

The country watered by these latter rivers is utterly waste, and contains no inhabitants.

The Zanskar rises in the extreme north of Lahoul, a little to the north-west of the Singo-la (pass), and with a south-easterly flow of over twenty miles, falls into the Bagha at Darcha. There are no signs of human habitation throughout its entire course.

There are other minor streams in Lahoul, which need no special notice, such as the Milang, that joins the Bagha below Darcha from the south-east, and the Baelung, with a great flow of water in the rainy season, that enters the same river at Baelung, a few miles above the junction of the Bagha and the Chundra.

The Sutledj can hardly be called one of the rivers of Kooloo, for it merely runs along the southern boundary of the subdivision for a distance of some thirty miles. It rises in Lake Manasorawa, about lat. 30° 35′ and long. 81° 35′. Up to its confluence with the Spiti river, Cunningham gives its length at 280 miles, with a fall of 33·8 feet per mile. Passing into the native state of Belaspore, it reaches Ropur, 560 miles from its source, when, taking an easterly direction for 120 miles, it flows a broad and mighty river by Loodiana and Philor, being joined by the Beas at Hari-ka-putun, beyond which, says Cunningham, its course is to the south-west for 400 miles to its junction with the Chenab opposite. The whole length of the Sutledj is 1,080 miles, or 130 miles more than that of the Chenab.

"On the 10th of November, 1762, the

shoulder of a vast mountain near Seoni fell into the river," to quote again from Cunningham, "and for forty days the stream was dammed up completely. People were stationed on the banks to give notice of the breaking of the barrier, which took place on the 19th of December of the same year. No lives were lost on this occasion, but a great deal of property was destroyed."

The one principal stream in Spiti is the river of the same name, which rises in the northern extremity of the district, at the foot of a snowy peak (K III.), 20,073 feet in height, and after a south-easterly course of ten miles, is joined from the south-west by the Lichu, that drains the mountains on either side of the Kunzum Pass.

The Spiti then turns to the east, and, in a very broad bed, the stream flowing in many channels, continues in the same direction for thirteen miles, receiving some considerable additions *en route*, when at this point it is joined by the Lagudarsi from the north, and turning to the south-east, with but one slight deflection to the west, approaches Mani, a distance of eighty-eight miles more, when it loses its broad bed, and with several twists, winds to the north-east, then again to the south-east, and close to Lari, the last village in Spiti, takes an easterly course into Bussahir, turning finally to the south, about five miles after quitting Spiti, and entering the Sutledj opposite the village of Khab; its complete length from source to mouth being estimated, in round numbers, at upwards of 120 miles, with a fall of over sixty feet per mile.

The length of the Spiti valley, from Losur village, where it first affords habitation for man, to Mani village, at the foot of the Manirung Pass, is about fifty miles, and there are other valleys, such as the Peen, the Parung, and the Lingti, which, with the continuation of the Spiti valley to the east, are all inhabited, though only in the parts which approach the main river. Besides these, there are several other valleys, which, from their elevation and the rigorous climate therein prevailing, could never be made available for human residence. Spiti, except at its most southern extremity, is entirely destitute of timber, though near Losur there are a few stunted willows and a scattered tree or so in a few of the villages; but the country is much wider and more open than in Lahoul; and the mountains ascend from the plain in gentle slopes. The landscape is, in truth, exceedingly striking, and the scenery in parts is very grand. From Kazeh to Dhunkur, for instance, the road, turning to the left, runs under some enormous clay pillars, the river sweeping onward in many a curve till lost to view behind projecting promontories; hills rise gradually to the left, and in hard and rugged outline to the right of the stream, and in the background lie a range of splendid snow-clad peaks, through which runs the Manirung Pass leading into Bussahir. Further down, a soil of clay and bold rock has to be traversed, from out of which uprise rough monumental-like masses that are not a little peculiar in appearance, for they are crenelated and honeycombed all over with deep holes and apertures, as if scooped out by art, supporting on their summits great boulders of stone, which, in all probability, have kept the masses underneath from wearing altogether away. "Along the course of the Spiti river" (to quote from a journal by Mr. Theobald, junior, published in the "Asiatic Society's Journal" for 1862) "are seen old river-terraces or deposits of shingle and sand, coarse and feebly stratified, and reaching to a height of some 400 feet above the present river-level. Behind these regular deposits, and both from beneath and also encroaching over them, rise almost mountainous accumulations of *débris*, precipitated by frost from the abruptly scarped limestone cliffs bounding the valley. The height of this gravelly mass mainly depends on that of the cliff at whose base it has accumulated, but not uncommonly reaches to 1,500 or 2,000 feet above the river." The most curious feature regarding the Spiti river is the extreme width of its bed, which, in places is nearly one mile in breadth, the stream itself, for the most part of its course, being both narrow and very shallow, and perfectly destitute of the boulders which, in the other rivers of the subdivision, are so numerous. "The bed of the Spiti river," says Captain Hay, "is so deep as to prevent its waters being any assistance to the people in cultivating; they depend entirely upon the small streams from the mountains feeding their '*kools*.'" * He also makes allusion to "the immense beds of *débris* forming plateaus of sometimes two miles in length, and from half to one mile in breadth, on which a quantity of calcareous deposit has been formed."

The tributaries of the Spiti are numerous, and of some size; but they flow, for the most part, through desolate tracts of country. From the north, the Kibjuna, the Tanmu, the Lagudarsi (the last rising in the Takling-la Pass), the Parung (from the Parung-la Pass), the Shilla, and the Lingti (over thirty miles in length, with a bed eighty yards in

---

* Watercourses.

width), fall into the Spiti on its left shore; while from the south come the Gyundi (over twenty miles in length), that rises at the foot of a snowy peak 21,772 feet in height; the Ratang, longer than the last, and one or two smaller streams, which all join the parent river in the upper portion of its course, and which perhaps might more appropriately be termed torrents. "Some of their beds are very remarkable, from 300 to 500 yards wide, quite straight and parallel, like the banks of a canal, and the *débris*, in some instances, from 200 to 300 feet above the water-level." —(Hay.)

The most important tributary of the Spiti is the Peen river, that rises in the most south-western point of Spiti, at the foot of what is marked in the map as "Snowy Peak No. 1," flowing in a north-easterly direction for nearly twenty miles, when it turns to the north, receiving many smaller rivulets on either side. For twenty-five miles more its course is north by east, receiving near Sungnum, ten miles from its mouth, the Parakio, or Parakees, which has had a line nearly parallel to its own, and which conveys about an equal volume of water. The width of the Peen, near its mouth, varies from 300 to 800 yards, and its length, from source to junction with the Spiti, above Dhunkur, is over forty-five miles. Nearly the whole course of the Peen and its tributaries is through a vast waste, where human foot has never trod.

The Beas rises at the crest of the Rohtung, 13,325 feet above the sea, and in its descent down the Kooloo side of the pass it is joined by other streams, and, with a course nearly due south, flows to Larjee, a distance in all of sixty-three miles, its fall up to this being 125·3 feet per mile. At Larjee it leaves Kooloo, and, turning to the south-west, enters Mundee, eventually joining the Sutledj at Hari-ka-Putun, near Ferozepore. Just below Bajoura, the Beas forms the boundary-line, for thirteen miles from this point to Larjee, between Mundee and Wuzeeri-Rupi. The entire length of the Beas is 350 miles. This noble river springs into existence from out a block of mica-slate on the summit of the Rohtung Pass, and from its very source forms a notable contrast to the Chundra, for almost from its infancy its course is marked by beauties of no mean order. Winding in a narrow rivulet over the pass which gives it birth, it is first brought prominently to notice as it plashes its puny stream over the rocky wall that runs athwart the line of the ascent of the Rohtung, and collecting more strength as it advances, it bears towards the foot of the pass, leaping over the boulders in its path, and being for a time lost to sight as it penetrates a line of cliffs that, thickly adorned with birch, hide it from view, till, in a thundering cascade above Ralla, it hurls itself, with a fall of over forty feet, into the narrow channel beneath. Forests of pine now engirt its banks, and, with many a turn and bend, it flows to the south towards a point between Ralla and Pulchan, where a sufficiently curious spectacle presents itself; for here the river plunges into a vast chasm, enclosed on either side by a precipitous barrier of rock not twenty feet apart, and often almost touching. It is with no small sensations of dread that one stands on the tottering rafters which connect the two shores; below roars the chafing stream, at a depth of upwards of 100 feet; the further one peers down, the more intense being the darkness, till faintly the surging foam of the fretting waters is to be perceived, as they dash with fury against the walls of the confining rock, and hasten away, in clashing tumult, to be lost as it were in the very bowels of the earth. For some 300 yards the Beas races through this almost subterranean passage, when it again bounds into the sunlight, its exit on the further side being most strikingly beautiful, seen as it is through a dense growth of woodland, that clings to either lofty cliff, and hangs over the river in a connecting arch. The Beas has now entered into the Kooloo, or Upper Beas valley, to which the noble stream has fittingly given its name. Descending lower, the Beas, confined in a compact bed, is encompassed on either side by scarped rocks, that appear as if they had been riven apart by some vast force of nature, at a period when the now petty rivulet was a mighty river, bearing everything before it.

In every nook where there is space, stand tier on tier of pines of every description common to these hills; while rising behind the opposite bank to the south are a line of cedars, which break the lower depths of the wooded mountains to the rear.

Two miles below, another river, larger than the Beas, joins it with an impetuous roar. This is the Serahi of the maps and the Beash Khund of the natives; for the Serahi is, in fact, but a small tributary of the latter. From this point of junction to close on Sooltanpore, a distance of about twenty-three miles, the Beas—its volume added to on either side by several feeders—presents a spectacle of beauty which can hardly be excelled; the river and the valley are in perfect harmony.

Sweeping down, in grand lines, come the mountains, covered almost to their summits with dense forests of *deodar, tosh, rae, kyle,** walnut, and plane, their sides broken by beetling cliff and rushing waterfall; while interspersed here and there are to be seen the homesteads of the peasantry, embowered in groves of mighty pine-trees, the Swiss-like architectural details of the houses bringing to one's mind scenes very far remote from the East. Most of the available ground for cultivation is laid out in fields, which rise in terraces, one over the other; but the monotony of these is relieved by the luxuriant vegetation, that breaks the hard lines of uniformity, and renders the waving crops but an additional feature in the landscape. Towering far over the hills which guard the valley, rise the mountains of the Snowy Range. To the north, over the Rohtung Pass, can be seen the jagged twin peaks of Gaphan, in Lahoul; to the north-east, across the Humta Pass, leading into Spiti, are the

---

* *Deodara excelsa, Picus Webbiana Abies Smithiana Pinus excelsa.*

Humta spurs; and to the west lie the Bara Banghal heights, some of which are never throughout the year entirely divested of snow. Below, through the centre of the valley, sweeps the Beas, with a never-ceasing roar. Bounding over rock and boulder, and separating here to tear round some pretty sylvan island, it joins its waters again on the further side, and rolling, tumbling, and frothing, with many an eddy, whirlpool, and rapid, it fights its way past Sooltanpore, where for the first time it begins to moderate its force. Journeying up the river, the road is hemmed in nearly the whole way by large trees that grow in great luxuriance, now and again occurring open, lawn-like plots, carpeted with the richest green grass.

Looking down the valley from Menalee, a rich prospect of hill and dale stretches out; and turn where one may, a series of most enchanting views are to be met with. Mountains rise over mountains, the great army of cedars becoming more and more scattered as the higher altitudes are approached, till there they disappear, and snowy ridges break the sky-line; nearer are thick forests of pine and cedar, which hold their own with a tenacious grasp on every knoll and coign of vantage, descending in serried phalanxes into the vales below, broken, or rather relieved, by masses of rock or more pleasantly by picturesque villages, hiding, like coy beauties, in the woodland that veils and yet enhances their charms. Range succeeds range, all alike lavishly endowed by the unsparing hand of nature, that has, in truth, appeared to have swept all the most winning aspects from the surrounding districts, but to lavish them with an abundant care upon the Upper Beas valley, where forest, waterfall, and river are all blended together by the soft, purply haze which hangs lightly over the lower reaches.

At Sooltanpore the Beas is a noble stream, and it gradually increases in width till it nears Bajoura, when it again narrows, and threads the vale that winds between Wuzeeri-Rupi on its left, and Mundee on its right bank. The aspect of the scenery now changes; the mountains crowd up in ascending precipices, that run down to the river's edge, many hundred feet below the road; and while, on the Mundee side, there are villages and a sprinkling of forest, on the other shore there is nought for the eye to rest on but steep grassy ascents, almost inaccessible to man or beast, and between Bajoura and Larjee, Dulashnee is the only village.

The Parbuttee, the largest affluent of the Beas, rises at the foot of Snowy Peak N (20,515 feet), and in the first part of its course runs in a north-westerly direction till joined by a stream of nearly equal dimensions from the north-east, when it sweeps round to the west, and, passing Manikurn, is joined, just below this, by the Malauna torrent, also from the north-east; and now turning to the south-west, it enters the Beas near Tia, halfway between Sooltanpore and Bajoura.

The Parbuttee, in its earlier stages, winds through a country which is the counterpart of that traversed by the Peen in Spiti, there being no signs of cultivation anywhere; but as Manikurn, fifty miles from its source, is approached, scattered villages appear, and the mountains become well wooded; and from this to its mouth, a distance of forty miles more, every available plot of ground is brought under the plough, while the forests become very extensive.

The scenery is wilder, and in some places more striking, than that in the Upper Beas valley, the snowy ranges to the east and south forming magnificent backgrounds to the beautiful glens that stretch upwards from the river-side; but although there are numerous forests, and the valley may be considered well timbered, yet there occur occasionally very large spaces that are either destitute of trees or cultivation, or are terraced with fields right down to the river, which again is not girt in so heavily with the alder and the deodar as is the Beas in Kooloo proper.

The crops in this valley are particularly fine, and it is, for its area, well populated.

The Surburi rises below "Snowy Peak 15,108," and flows in a south-easterly direction for thirty miles, past Kuronw rest-house, to Sooltanpore, entering the Beas immediately to the south of that town. It is so far a noticeable stream, as it runs along the Main Trade Line down the Bubboo Pass. The Surburi valley is very much shut in, the enclosing mountains rising to a considerable altitude on either side, the range on the left bank being sparsely clothed with timber, which, however, is sufficiently plentiful on the opposite shore. There are not many villages in the valley, which in several places presents some fine points of scenery.

The Hoorl rises in the lower spurs of the range that divides Spiti from Wuzeeri-Rupi, and with a south-westerly course of thirty-five miles, enters the Beas just opposite Bajoura. The features of the valley through which this stream flows are much the same as those of the Parbuttee valley.

The river Larjee descends from the western flank of Snowy Peak No. 1, from which the Peen, in Spiti, takes its rise on the other side.

This is a considerable stream, nearly as large as the Parbuttee, and has a course in an easterly direction of nearly seventy-five miles, joining the Beas at Larjee, twenty-three miles to the south of Sooltanpore. The Larjee is met by several smaller torrents, the one that falls into it near Tagwarcha village from the north-west, twenty miles from its junction with the Beas, being of some size. It forms the boundary between Wuzeeri-Rupi and Seoraj. The Larjee valley has many features in common with that of the Parbuttee, but it is narrower and less thickly populated.

The Tirthan rises to the south-west of Snowy Peak No. 1, between Spiti and Seoraj, and for the first thirty-two miles flows to the south-west, when, being met by a considerable tributary at Bundul village, it bears away to the north-west, and, passing Plach, after an entire course of sixty-two miles, enters the Larjee stream at Larjee;

for the last eighteen miles, or from Munglor to Larjee, forming the boundary between Mundee and Seoraj. Near Plach it is joined by the Chata from the south-east, and at Munglor by the Bah, which have each a course of over twenty miles, the latter stream being the continuation of the frontier line between Seoraj and Mundee.

For the first twenty-five miles the Tirthan passes through a sterile country, but then the valley lowers, and villages become numerous ; but the scenery throughout is nowhere equal to that found in the line of the Beas or the Parbuttee. There are, however, some considerable ranges of forest, and this part of Seoraj is densely inhabited. From Plach to Larjee the Tirthan passes through a very narrow vale, and, as Larjee is neared, the villages are far between and high up above the roadway, while the forests disappear altogether, giving place to bare stretches of grass.

The Arni river rises in the southern spurs of the Jalouri range, in Seoraj, and, after a south-westerly course of nearly thirty miles, joins the Bisna, close to Tumun village. The scenery of the country watered by the Arni deserves no especial comment. There are many considerable forests, and villages are numerous; but the landscape has not many features of interest.

The Bisna, in Seoraj, rises to the south of the Jalouri range, immediately opposite the Bah, that runs into the Tirthan at Munglor, and, flowing south, forms, for ten miles, the boundary-line between Seoraj and Mundee, and, for the remaining fourteen of its course, between the former and Sookhet, it is joined by the Arni, which has a larger volume than its own, at Tumun, and enters the river Sutledj between the villages of Fareenoo and Banoo.

The Kurpan is a considerable stream, forty miles in length, which, rising to the south of the Jalouri range, flows almost due south, joining the Sutledj opposite Datnagar, in Bussahir. The scenery of the Kurpan valley closely resembles that of the Arni, but there are fewer forests, and perhaps less cultivation.

The Kunrad is an unimportant stream; but, in its south-easterly course of fifteen miles, it forms the boundary-line between Seoraj and Bussahir, entering the Sutledj opposite the hamlet of Sha, in Bussahir.

The Solung, or Beash Khund, rises at the foot of the peak "M" (20,356 feet), on the Rohtung range, and has a south-easterly course of about thirteen miles, joining its waters with those of the Beas at Pulchan. In the Solung valley there is but one village, famous for its deodar-tree, said to be the largest in India. The scenery in this valley exceeds in grandeur anything that can be found elsewhere in Kooloo. The river in a swift current courses between mountains clad in impenetrable forests, from the midst of which jut out vast headlands of perpendicular rock; and, about three miles above Pulchan, a series of similar gigantic cliffs, over 600 feet in height, rise up sheer from the river, and line its course for a considerable distance. Approached through beautiful glades of ancient pines and horse-chestnuts, the valley comes at last into view, bowered with forests on either shore, while to the rear stand forth, in indescribable majesty, the tremendous heights of the Snowy Range, which here mount to upwards of 20,000 feet above sea-level.

The landscape in the Solung valley is, in my opinion, unsurpassable, and certainly unmatched by anything in the rest of the subdivision.

## CHAPTER III.

**Communications.—Rivers, Passes, Roads, Bridges, Ferries, Bungalows, Rest-houses.**

THE track through Kooloo and Lahoul has been used for a lengthened period by traders between the Punjab and Ladakh, but no particular attention was devoted to this line until Mr. Davies, then secretary to the Punjab Government, in 1862 issued his Trade Report, and drew attention to the advantages that might accrue from fostering this commerce. Subsequently the main line was, to a certain extent, improved, and by 1863 a better pathway had been laid over the Rohtung Pass, a *sungha* bridge being thrown over the Chundra in Lahoul, at a spot where previously there had only been a *jhula* or rope bridge. For some time afterwards, there were apparently but few efforts made to improve the existing communications; but in 1865, Mr. Forsyth, Commissioner of the Jullundur division, reported favourably on the advisability of extending the existing road, and, since 1866, various sums have been allowed from the Imperial revenue for this undertaking. It is worthy of record, too, that the Rajah of Mundee presented the munificent donation of £10,000, with a view to having that part of the line which passes through Mundee (between Kangra and Kooloo) brought into working order.

A new route was projected over the Bubboo Pass into Kooloo, and the communications in Lahoul were also taken in hand, rest-houses and serais being erected as far as funds would allow. For 1870-1871 the sum of 5,000 rupees has been allowed for the Lahoul road, and 5,000 rupees for the works on the Rohtung Pass road, and these operations, carried on under the able superintendence of Mr. Theodore, are fast approaching to completion.

The arrangements for the labour-supply were as follows. Willing workmen could not be had, and, pursuing the precedent of 1863, each *kothee* in Kooloo had to give so many men, amounting in all to 400, who worked for fifteen days, and received for that period two rupees per man. Some of the *zemindars* had to come from long distances, but it has so happened that those who lived furthest off, and whose services have been utilized by the State, are hardly ever called upon to do the Begar,* which falls heavily on the *kothees* in the Upper Beas valley; and therefore the burden on all has been more equal than might have been expected; nor is it, in my opinion, a bad political measure to now and then exact from the *zemindars* something that will suffice to show there is a paramount power, whose will must be obeyed.

All the works on this line cannot be completed this season. The new Rohtung Pass road is now ready, but the new *sungha,* opposite Koksur village, cannot be com-

* Forced labour.

menced this year, for some time must be allowed for the drying of the timbers, which have, in addition, to be dragged from Kooloo over the pass to the point selected for the bridge. This year also, certain settlement operations have necessitated the presence of each *zemindar* at his homestead until the autumn was far advanced; and it thus became impracticable to attempt the transport of the trees to the point selected for the bridge. For the transit of the logs nearly 2,000 porters will be required, and, with the late heavy pressure there has been on the people, I think this work must stand over till next season. Nor do I consider that it is absolutely necessary to have another bridge at Koksur: the new road over the pass is connected with the older line, and though the distance from Koksur, in Lahoul, to Ralla, in Kooloo, by the former, is greater than by the latter, yet in point of time there would be a saving, in consequence of the greater facilities for getting quickly over the ground.

The Lahoul road has been pressed on, but there are many obstacles to the speedy advance to completion of this work. The population is scanty, and the line of country through which the communications pass is very difficult, nor are the labourers that can be procured worth much. Fair progress has, however, been made, and all the credit for this is entirely and solely due to Mr. Theodore, whose unremitting attention to his duties in a country so desolate and so bitterly cold as is Lahoul, will not, I trust, be forgotten. Literally, for weeks at a time, has Mr. Theodore been living almost at the top of the Rohtung, over 13,000 feet in height, and, undaunted either by the desertion of his servants, the disobedience and impertinence of the workmen, and the rigours of the climate, he has, on a salary of 200 rupees a month, done the work that could not have been better performed by a Government engineer on double the salary. The expenditure for the year, on the roads in Lahoul and near the

Rohtung, will be furnished in a separate paper.

I now proceed to treat on the principal lines of communication in this subdivision.

The Main Trade Line, commencing at the crest of the Bubboo, passes Kuronw and Sooltanpore, and winds by the left bank of the Beas up to Menalee; shortly after crossing the Solung it ascends to Ralla, and, traversing the Rohtung, descends by the new road to a spot opposite to Koksur village. It then turns up the left bank of the Chundra, and near Koksur rest-house passes to the right shore, following the course of the river till it is joined by the Bagha. The path now lies over this last stream, and along its right bank past Kielung, Kolung, and Darcha to Putseo, where it changes to the left side of the river; and just beyond Zingzingbar, the last encampment at the foot of the Bara Lacha, again leads back to the right bank, and so ascends the pass, from thence proceeding into Ladakh by Lingtee.

All throughout Kooloo this road is in

excellent order for mule traffic; the gradients are easy, and the pathway from ten to twelve feet wide; and both over the Rohtung and for various portions of the line through Lahoul, it is easily traversible by baggage animals; but, as it nears the Bara Lacha, the path becomes lost in boulders, and speedy locomotion is impossible.

The larger and better bridges, all *sunghas*, are the following:—

One at Sooltanpore, over the Surburi torrent, that descends from the Bubboo Pass.

A smaller one than the above, near Katrain village, over a hill stream that joins the Beas lower down.

One of similar size, north of Menalee, over the Menalee stream. This was carried bodily away in July, but was replaced the following month, the new bridge being sixty-four feet in width.

One near Pulchan, five miles from Menalee, over the Solung river. This is a large bridge, and spans two separate portions of the stream.

The Kootlee bridge (between the foot of the Rohtung Pass and Koksur rest-house) over the Chundra is ninety-eight feet in span: the upper scantlings have to be removed every winter.

At the villages of Koksur, Gondla, and Tandee, in Lahoul, there are *jhula* or rope bridges, which connect the main line with tracks on the opposite shore.

One over the Bagha, opposite Tandee, in Lahoul, at its junction with the Chundra.

One over the Bagha, at Keilung, connecting the latter village with Kardung, on the left bank of the river.

The Zanskar bridge, over the Zanskar river, that joins the Bagha just below Darcha. This was swept away this year (1870), but has been replaced.

The Putseo bridge of beams, with slates for the roadway, close to Putseo encampment, on the left bank of the Bagha.

The bridge over the Tserap river, the boundary between Cashmere and British territory.

There is a poor rest-house and a wooden serai at Kuronw, on the Kooloo side of the Bubboo: both these, though built but a few months ago, are in very bad order.

At Sooltanpore there is a good rest-house, that has been recently done up, and a serai of some size was completed in January, 1870.

There is no rest-house at Menalee, but a serai of three small rooms was erected early in the present year.

At Pulchan and Ralla there are small rest-houses, but no serais, and halfway up the Rohtung Pass, at Murree, there is a small shieling, built by Lehna Sing, the Sikh, and still called after him: this last structure is almost a ruin.

Koksur, on the Lahoul side of the Rohtung Pass, boasted once of an excellent rest-house, with out-offices, but, exposed as the building is to the depredations of traders, it is now in bad order, having been denuded of all ironwork, and the windows of their panes of glass.

At Darcha there is only a serai.

Serais are to be erected at the villages of Koksur, Sissoo, Gondla, Kielung, and Kolung, in Lahoul, and at the encampment of Putseo and Zingzingbar; but there are great difficulties in the way of getting these buildings prepared, in a country where labour is so difficult to procure and timber so scarce, and often so very far distant from the point where it is required.

The line next in importance is the one which proceeds from Sooltanpore to Simla. This passes down the right bank of the Beas to below Bajoura, and then crosses to the other side of the river, and enters Wuzeeri-Rupi. At Larjee the Beas turns off to the south-west; the road then follows the Tirthan for twelve or thirteen miles, through Mundee and Seoraj, and leaving that stream just below Plach, ascends the Jalouri Pass, and, turning in a southerly direction, reaches Dulash, the last Kooloo village, which is seven or eight miles from the Sutledj, Simla being five and a half marches from this point.

This may be termed a capital road throughout, with the exception of a small portion that passes through Mundee, the gradients in which are badly laid out, and the last final dip to the Sutledj from Dulash, where the track is susceptible of improvement, and is always much injured in the rains.

The Bajoura bridge is now in course of construction, the river Beas being, at the point of crossing, 180 feet in breadth. For the present a ferry connects the two shores.

The Larjee bridge is of some size, and spans a formidable stream that separates Larjee, in Seoraj, from Wuzeeri-Rupi.

There is another considerable bridge over the Tirthan river, three miles beyond Larjee, which connects the Mundee and Kooloo Seoraj's.

The Munglor bridge, close to Munglor village, is of some size, though only over a hill stream; on either shore are the Mundee and Kooloo Seoraj's.

The Sutledj bridge is between Dulash, in Kooloo, and Kotghur; it is 200 feet in span, and has only this year (1870) been again rebuilt.

There are, throughout the entire road to Simla, no serais, with the exception of the one at Sooltanpore, before alluded to.

At Bajoura, ten miles to the south of Sooltanpore, there is a comfortable rest-house.

Larjee, fourteen miles below Bajoura, is provided with a double-roomed native building, which serves as a shelter to travellers; it is a very poor structure, and, when funds are available, a proper rest-house should be erected.

At Jebee, on the Kooloo side of the Jalouri Pass, there is a small rest-house.

Additional rest-houses are required at Larjee, Munglor, and Dulash; they could be run up at an expenditure of 500 rupees apiece.

Besides the main line in the Upper Beas valley, there is another that is equally good along the left bank of the Beas. This adheres to the main line as far as Dobee (eleven miles from Sooltanpore), and then crosses to the other side of the river, passing Nuggur and Jugutsookh *en route*, joining the main line again at Menalee.

An excellent *sungha* bridge, with a span of upwards of ninety feet, crossed the Beas just opposite Dobee, but on the 31st July last it was carried away in an unprecedented rise of the river, which brought down an accumulation of timber that completely destroyed one of the piers, and resulted in the destruction of the fabric. This bridge should be rebuilt lower down the river.

For the present, the Nuggur bridge, three miles higher up, with a span of 110 feet, is the main means of communication between the two shores. This bridge was also much damagèd by the flood, but it stood the shock, and is now perfectly safe.

The Dwangan bridge is between Nuggur and Jugutsookh, and close to the latter village it crosses a very furious torrent.

The Menalee bridge, over the Beas, is between Jugutsookh and Menalee, and is seventy-eight feet in span.

Between Nuggur and Menalee there is also the Kelat bridge over the Beas, which gives a means of passage from the "Main Trade Line" to either Nuggur or Jugutsookh. This bridge is very old, and should be renewed.

There are no serais or rest-houses on this line.

From Sooltanpore there are two roads up the Parbuttee valley. The first crosses the Beas, ascends the Bijli-Mahdeo hill, and, passing by Tipri village, turns up the left bank of the Parbuttee to Jhirree and Manikurn; the second line going south from Sooltanpore to Shumshee village, and, the Beas being passed, joining the other near Jhirree.

There is a large bridge over the Beas at Sooltanpore, between the latter place and the village of Dart.

Tipri bridge is over the Parbuttee, between Tipri and Jhirree.

The Kushole bridge over the Parbuttee is between Kushole and Manikurn.

There is a ferry over the Beas near Shumshee, which leads to the village of Buin, on the right bank of the Parbuttee, on to the opposite shore, from whence the road goes to Jhirree.

The main Spiti line commences at Losur, on the right bank of the Spiti river, and, crossing the stream at Khiotto, turns up over a low pass, and touches at Khibur, from which, again descending, it continues along the same side to Dhunkur, a distance of about forty-five miles; the entire road being very good, except where it traverses the bed of the Spiti river, and betweeen Khibur and Kazeh, where it has been injured by landslips.

At Losur the Spiti is crossed by a *jhula* bridge over fifty feet in span.

Near Khiotto there is a *jhula* bridge over the Spiti. This is off the main road.

Almost opposite Rangri there is a *sungha;* this is over the Spiti, off the main road, lying between Khibur and Kazeh.

The Dhunkur *sungha* is seventy feet in

span, crosses the Spiti river two miles to the north of Dhunkur, and leads to the Peen valley and the Babeh Pass.

A small rest-house has been this year erected at Losur, and a room in the fort at Dhunkur is usually placed at the disposal of travellers in the valley.

The road from Plach to Nirmand, in Seoraj, is a fairly good one, but is little used by Europeans; it leaves Plach just off the main Simla line, near Munglor, and winds over the Busloh Pass to Nirmand, close to the river Sutledj. In distance it is forty-five miles.

The Lower Beas valley road is connected with Sooltanpore by the bridge over the Beas, near the town, and, proceeding south, winds below the Bijli-Mahdeo hill to Buin; here it crosses the Parbuttee, and continues along the left bank of the Beas till the Jhirree ferry, on the main Simla line, is reached. In length it is about twenty-two miles.

The Jheea *sungha* bridge is over the

Parbuttee, and close to the junction of that river with the Beas, between Buin and Jheea.

The Malauna Pass road leads from Manikurn, in the Parbuttee valley, along the right bank of the Parbuttee, and at Chulaul village ascends the Kundee Pass, touches at Malauna, and then crosses the Malauna Pass, emerging at Nuggur, in the Upper Beas valley.

There is a good *sungha* bridge over the Malauna stream, just before the village of the same name is reached.

The road from Kooloo to Spiti leaves Jugutsookh, on the left bank of the Beas, and, passing the village of Prini, commences the ascent of the Humta Pass, up the Raini torrent, and, surmounting that pass, enters on the Chundra valley, the encamping-grounds of Chaitroo, Futtehrooneh, and Karchee following each other in succession. From the latter the line crosses the Kunzum Pass, and leads to Losur, in Spiti, a distance in all of some sixty miles.

There are no rivers along this route, but

many of the hill streams are most furious torrents, which can hardly be forded after the sun has melted the ice-beds by which they are supplied.

The line passes over the Shigri glacier, between Futtehrooneh and Karchee.

The Upper Chundra valley line leaves the Bara Lacha Pass at the point where the Chundra first comes into notice, and follows the course of the stream along its left bank for four marches, to a high pass, from the crest of which commences the boundary of Spiti. Below the pass runs the Lichee stream, which is fordable, and from this Losur is six miles distant. The length of this most execrable road is over fifty miles.

The Chundra Bagha line leaves the "Main Line" at the bridge over the Bagha, near the junction of the latter with the Chundra, and, keeping to the right bank of the united streams for fifteen miles, enters Chumba territory, between the villages of Jolung and Tirot.

The Manirung Pass line leaves Dhunkur,

and, descending south, crosses the Spiti river eight miles below, and, touching Mani village, on the right bank of the stream, ascends to the crest of the Manirung Pass, a distance of twenty miles more. This road is a mere track.

At Mani village there is usually a *jhula* bridge annually thrown over the Spiti.

The Peen valley road commences at Dhunkur, and, crossing the Spiti river, keeps to the left bank of the Peen, a tributary of the latter, for about eighteen miles, when it takes the right side of the stream as far as Buldun encamping-ground; it then turns due south, and follows the upward course of a hill stream to Lursa encamping-ground, at the foot of the Babeh, and so passes into Bussahir. The length of this road is about sixty-five miles. The bridge that connects the Peen valley with Dhunkur has been alluded to before.

The Kwagur Pass road leaves Dhunkur by the path to the Manirung Pass, but quits it again at the Spiti, along the left bank of which river it continues for fourteen miles, till at Lari, the last village in Spiti, it crosses the stream, and leads over the Kwagur Pass into Shealkur, in Bussahir. The road is simply a track, but it is the one most used by travellers from Simla into Spiti.

At Lari village there is generally to be found a *jhula* over the Spiti.

The road over the Parang-la to Ladakh leaves the main Spiti line between Khiotto and Khiebar, and crosses the Parang-la almost immediately after.

The Solung valley road leaves the "Main Trade Line" at Pulchan, in the Upper Beas valley, and turns up the right bank of the Solung river, until all further progress is stopped by the mountains.

Before proceeding to give an account of the passes in the subdivision, it may not be out of place to shortly describe the *sungha* and *jhula* bridges.

A *sungha* bridge is formed as follows:—

On either side the river piers of rubble masonry, laced with cross-beams of timber, are built up; and into these are inserted stout poles, one over the other in successively projecting tiers, the interstices between the latter being filled up with cross-beams. The projecting poles increase in size as they approach the upper platform, and have a slight incline upwards, their shore ends being firmly braced into the stonework. Between the uppermost row of timbers, two or three long and very strong connecting trees are placed, and scantlings are laid over them for the pathway, in some cases a railing being added for greater security. *Sungha* bridges are sometimes of considerable span; and, if well built, last from thirty to forty years.

A *jhula* bridge is fashioned with ropes of birch or willow twigs. "The supports are two stout cables, each composed of some twelve or fifteen small ropes, stretched over rude piers on either bank at about five feet apart, and finally secured by being buried deeply beneath the stones forming the piers. Between the main cables, and about two feet below them, a third of smaller dimensions is stretched, and supported by tight ropes passed over the side cables."—(Theobald.)

*Jhula* bridges are not usually allowed to remain all the year round, and are mostly only put up for the convenience of villages separated by some river. When new, they are quite safe, as between the main cables and the footway there is a rough rope lacing; but they soon get worn, and then, to any one who has not much nerve, they are exceedingly dangerous; and Cunningham mentions that he has seen Ladakh women sit down in the middle of one of these structures, and actually scream with terror!

The Bara Lacha Pass, variously estimated at from 16,221 to 16,500 feet above sea-level, is in Lahoul, lying between Zingzingbar and Lingti encamping-grounds, and across it runs the "Main Trade Line" to Ladakh. It is generally open for traffic by the beginning or middle of June, and remains so till October, although it can be, and constantly is, crossed in May, and even in

December; but from the latter month to the end of April it is hermetically sealed. The ascent of this pass from the Lahoul side is almost imperceptible; and were the road good, the gradient is so easy that wheeled conveyances might be drawn over it. The last halting-place, Zingzingbar, is nearly 14,000 feet above sea-level, so that the rise to the crest of the pass is by no means great. The road goes up the course of the Bagha, skirts the Seoraj-dul, a clear sheet of water about three-quarters of a mile in circumference, and then winds over the summit, descending by an easy slope to the plains on the other side.

In July, August, and September the Bara Lacha is almost entirely divested of snow. From the crest another path turns to the south towards the head of the Chundra valley; but this is a mere track, and one, too, which, without a guide, it is not safe to traverse. It winds for about three miles between lofty peaks of dazzling snow, and then commences to dip down towards the Chundra river, and is certainly not a practicable route for laden animals.

The Bara Lacha Pass is so confined between the surrounding heights, that the view from it is necessarily a limited one.

The Shingo-la (16,772 feet), otherwise termed the Zanskar Pass, is situated at the head of the Zanskar ravine, and is occasionally used by petty traders between Lahoul and Zanskar, in Ladakh.

The Goonthal Pass lies between Goondla and Kielung, and is 14,993 feet in height. The ascent on the Goondla side is easy, lying over grassy plains; but the descent to Kielung (reached by a *sungha* bridge over the Bagha) is both abrupt and difficult. A little trouble would make this a good traffic-route, and so dispense with the journey along the treacherous soil that flanks the present lower road between Kielung and Goondla. The mountain across which this pass occurs is held in veneration by the people, numerous cairns of stones having been built on its summit by devout pilgrims. From the

Goonthal Pass a very extensive view is obtained.

From the Chundra Bagha valley two paths ascend the mountains on the left bank of the river, which, by the Bara Banghal and Kooktee passes, enter the district of Bara Banghal, and from thence go on to Kangra. Both these passes are over 17,000 feet in height, and are excessively difficult for the pedestrian, and for laden animals are quite impracticable.

The Kwagur Pass is between the villages of Soomrah, in Bussahir, and Lari, in Spiti, and occurs on the line from Dhunkur to Simla. It is an easy pass, and not a high one, being between 14,000 and 15,000 feet above sea-level.

The Manirung Pass, with the Spiti village of Mani on one side and Robuk in Bussahir on the other, is given by Mr. Theobald, junior, at 18,889 feet in height. "The ascent from the Simla side is very steep, and extremely laborious, from the heaps of loose débris one is forced to climb over. . . . On gaining the snow-bed, near the summit, the path was much easier, although the snow was rather slippery" (this was on the 3rd August, 1861), "and there were a few crevasses to be avoided," the descent lying over a glacier much finer and larger than the one on the south side. "The glacier," continues Mr. Theobald, "on the north face of the pass, terminated in a sheer wall of ice, from beneath which a muddy torrent was springing, and the lateral moraine over which the road descended was but little less abrupt." The Manirung, or Robuk-la, as it is locally termed, is a good deal used by traders between Spiti and Bussahir, and occasionally by English tourists from Simla. It is open from May till October.

The road to the Babeh Pass strikes off from the Sutledj at the Wangto bridge, ascending to the valley of Gutgaon, in Bussahir, the first village in Spiti, after the crossing, being Modh, in the Peen valley. This pass is open from May till October, and is mainly used by Bussahir and Spiti traders.

Mr. Theobald, junior, who crossed the Babeh on 1st September, 1861, remarks that the "ascent from Spiti is far from difficult, though a large glacier descends from the summit. This glacier is fissured by numerous crevasses, stretching nearly across it, and at short intervals from one another. Few of the crevasses are so broad as to be impassable; but in order to select the best spot for crossing, the road winds considerably, and it would be decidedly difficult to cross without a guide who knew the track." On the descent to Bussahir a small glacier has to be traversed, and the march down is extremely steep, ending in "a region of birches and verdure."

The Parung-la is quoted by Theobald, who went over it on the 13th of August, 1861, at 19,132 feet above sea-level; Cunningham, however, places its altitude at 18,502 feet. This is, in all probability, the loftiest pass in British territory, and all who have journeyed across it agree as to its extreme difficulty. The Parung-la is between the village of Khiebur, in Spiti, and Ladakh. "On the ascent to the pass," says Theobald, "a little snow is met with in hollows and in sheltered places, but the road is free of snow to the summit. The crest of the pass is a rocky ridge of vertical limestone strata, forming a gap between high snowy peaks on either hand. From this rocky ridge one steps off on to a fine glacier, which is seen filling up the valley beneath, and which is mainly augmented by the gradual descent of lateral glaciers and ice, from the high snowy peaks to the west. Few crevasses exist in this glacier, and the descent over it is gradual and easy, though there are some awkward bits of road just after quitting it, where the ground is very steep, and the road creeps along the chasm that yawns between the mountain-side on one hand and the glacier on the other, and which is produced by the melting of the glacier in contact with the dark, warm rocks of the valley."

This pass is much used by traders between Ladakh, Bussahir, and Spiti, and occasionally by tourists proceeding from Simla to Leh, on the Pangong lake. The Parung-la is open from June till October, but is dangerous at all times, as it is liable to severe snowstorms even in summer, the bones of the numerous dead animals to be found on the line of the ascent attesting to the difficulty of its passage.

The road to the Takling-la (over 17,000 feet) strikes off from Spiti, between the villages of Hull and Quito, and enters Ladakh. This pass is very seldom used.

The Koonzum Pass is on the high road, between the Upper Chundra valley and Losur, in Spiti. From the Spiti side the ascent is almost *nil*, the crest of the pass being but a few hundred feet above the main elevation of the Spiti valley.

In the descent to the Chundra river it is, however, pretty steep, but by no means difficult. The Koonzum Pass is open from May till October, but it is frequently crossed as late as December. Its height is over 14,900 feet.

The Rohtung Pass, between Ralla, in Kooloo, and Koksur, in Lahoul, on the Main Trade Line, is 13,325 feet in height, and a good road for traffic goes along its west side. From Ralla the ascent is rather steep, but the descent into Lahoul is by an easy gradient. The crest of the Rohtung is over a mile in length, and the pass is open from the end of April to the end of December; but in the early summer, and again towards the autumn, it is liable to severe snowstorms, accompanied with a deadly cold wind; and it was in such a storm that seventy-two *coolies* [labourers] lost their lives in October, 1862. These men were returning from the bridge-works at Koksur, in Lahoul, and, though the snow lay then deep all over the mountains, the sky was clear; but, in the act of crossing, a furious gale sprung up, and drove the snow in great drifts over the unfortunate people, who were choked and smothered as they stood. Some of their number managed to escape by keeping their heads to the wind and lying on the ground, extricating themselves shortly after; but these were only the men who were accustomed to the vagaries of the pass. The bodies of the dead were not recovered for some days after.

Lord Elgin, when Governor-General, crossed the Rohtung in 1863, and recrossed it again the same day, a feat that few Englishmen would care to undertake; and it is said the great exertions necessary on this occasion brought on an aggravation of the disease of heart complaint, which shortly after led to this lamented statesman's demise. The pass, it may be said, is never quite closed altogether, as Lahoulees cross it in fine weather even in January and February, when the snow lies thirty feet deep on its summit. The river Beas takes its rise on this pass, and at the spot, Beas Ricki, where it emerges from the mountain, an open enclosure was erected, about 1840, by Lehna Sing, the Sikh governor of Kooloo: halfway up the Kooloo side of the pass there is also a small rest-house, built by the order of the same individual. The views from the top of the Rohtung are not extensive, but the whole line of heights along the right bank of the Chundra is very fine, as are also the peaks of the Shigri, to the east.

The Humta Pass rises between Preenee, in the Upper Beas valley, and the encamping of Chaitroo, a desolate spot in the Upper Chundra valley. The ascent of the pass, estimated at over 15,000 feet in altitude, is somewhat long and tedious, but the scenery throughout is very beautiful. Commencing at Preenee village, the road rises by a steep incline for about a mile, and then wanders for twelve miles more through rich forests of pine and walnut, interspersed with open grassy slopes, swept bare of trees by the avalanches, to Chikkun, at the foot of the pass, just above which vegetation dies out, and now frowning precipices of limestone, heavily crested with snow, which spreads over the roadway, form the landmarks of the line over the mountain. The view from the crest is superb; on one side lies the Kooloo valley, in all its sylvan beauty, and, turning from this aspect of wealthy woodland and extensive area of cultivation, on the other side we are confronted by the snowy heights, which tower over one another in dazzling brilliancy. Although much higher than the Rohtung, the Humta, if not easier, is a pleasanter pass to traverse, and it is but little troubled with the furious icy gales which rage on the other. The descent into the Chundra valley is somewhat abrupt, and crosses two beds of snow, which have to be carefully threaded. The Humta is open from May till the end of October; and, if the weather holds up, it can be traversed even in December.

The Malauna Pass, over 12,000 feet in height, is between the villages of Nuggur and Malauna, and the ascent on either side is most fatiguing. This pass is seldom used except by shepherds, who take over their flocks; but occasionally parties of Englishmen cross it on their way to inspect the curious village of Malauna (mention of which is made elsewhere). If the Humta Pass ranks first for its stately grandeur and wondrous beauty, the Malauna is certainly pre-eminent for the marvellous views of snowy mountains procurable from its summit; and such an extensive range of peak on peak, and mile on mile of glacier, can hardly be matched from any other vantage-ground.

The Bubboo Pass, 10,000 feet above the sea-level, is on the Main Trade route, and its crest is on the boundary-line between Mundee State and Kooloo, the nearest villages being Budwanee, on the Mundee side, and Kuronw on the other. The ascent and descent are by steep gradients, the road being an excellent one throughout. In the rajah's territory the hill is somewhat bare of vegetation near the summit, but from the crest of the pass to Kuronw the path winds through dense forest. The Bubboo is closed with snow during January, February, and March.

The Bajoura Pass, about 7,000 feet in height, is between Kamand, in Mundee, and

Bajoura, in the Beas valley. At one time the regular trade route lay over this pass, but of late it has fallen almost into disuse, except in the winter, when the Bubboo is closed. The ascent from Mundee is very rugged and steep, and winds over bare hills; but on the other flank the path passes through a fine grove of trees. The Bajoura can hardly be considered a Kooloo pass, as it lies almost entirely in the Mundee State, the boundaries of which run close by Bajoura.

The Jalouri Pass, 10,500 feet in height, lies between Munglor and Kot, in Seoraj, on the Simla line of road. It is a very beautiful pass, being richly wooded on both sides, and the path over it is, unless just after "the rains," always in excellent order. Some very fine views of the Snowy Range are to be had in the ascent from Munglor, and from the crest, which is quite bare of timber, the whole valley of the Sutledj, with the Simla mountains, comes into view. The Jalouri is closed in the winter months.

The Busloh Pass, 11,000 feet above sea-level, is on the same range as the Jalouri, and occurs on the road from Plach to Nirmand, in Seoraj, and is much the same in its general features as the one last referred to, being densely wooded; the road over it is, however, but an indifferent one.

## CHAPTER IV.

**Administrative Staff.—The Assistant-Commissioner.—The Tehsildars.—Deputy-Inspectors of Police.—Head of Royal House of Kooloo.—Chiefs of Lahoul and Spiti. — Negees. — Gyatpos. — Lumberdars. — Chowkeydars.— Putwarries. —Marriage Registrars. —Crime and Litigation.—Frequent Changes of Judicial and other Officers deprecated.—Appointment of Kooloo Men to Government Posts advocated.**

WHEN the province of Kooloo fell into the hands of the British, in 1846, it was attached to the Deputy-Commissionership of Kangra, which again forms one of the three districts of the Jullundur division. But, although nominally a portion of Kangra, it was, both from its extensive area of over 6,000 square miles, and its population of close on 100,000, practically a separate charge; and the Assistant-Commissioner, under whose care the subdivision was placed, was entrusted with more freedom of action than is usually granted to such a subordinate official. And there were many good reasons why this should be so; for the territory over which the Assistant-Commissioner ruled was nearly as large as that governed by the sovereigns of Kooloo in the palmiest days of that monarchy, and comprised within its area three races, which may be deemed distinct, if consideration be given to the fact of the diverse creeds, languages, and customs, that distinguish the several phases of the population. Again, it was next to impossible for the Deputy-Commissioner to even visit the country, and in no instance up to date has any one Deputy-Commissioner been able, in his tour of office, to inspect the separate valleys of Kooloo, Lahoul, and Spiti, the control of which has been perforce vested in the hands of his Assistant, whose wishes and suggestions formed the guide for any action on the part of his superior.

The first Assistant-Commissioner was Captain Hay, who held the appointment as a permanency; but, on his resigning office, it became the custom to depute an officer every summer to Kooloo, who generally entered the valley in May and quitted it again in October. On my being gazetted to Kooloo, I took an early opportunity of urging the advisability of the appointment of Assistant-Commissioner being continued for at least two years; that the Assistant-Commissioner should stay, for the whole of that period, in Kooloo, and not be drafted in the winter, as had hitherto been the rule, to Dhurmsala, thus leaving the country in the care of a Tehsildar,* who became perfectly independent; and that appellate powers, both in criminal and civil cases, should be entrusted to the officer in charge, as, from the distance of the valley from Dhurmsala, the inaccessibility of the latter in the winter, and the ignorance of the Kooloo people of any tongue but their own, they were practically debarred from ever appeal-

* A subordinate native official, who sees to the collection of revenue, and is invested with certain magisterial powers.

ing at all. His Honour the Lieutenant-Governor saw fit, on these representations, to constitute Kooloo a two years' appointment; and, while granting the Assistant-Commissioner appellate powers on the criminal side, he obtained from the Supreme Government the passing of Act IV. of 1870, which enabled the Assistant-Commissioner to entertain appeals on the civil side also.

Thus the Assistant-Commissioner, for the future, will, of necessity, be an officer of some standing, for, to exercise the powers that, as Assistant-Commissioner of Kooloo, he must *ex officio* wield, he must have passed all the necessary legal examinations; and it is not to be supposed that appellate powers would be entrusted to any one who had not been for three or four years in the Commission. This retention, also, of office for two years, and his continued stay in the valley for the whole of that period, will obviate the difficulty that before existed, which resulted in complaints, that just as an Assistant-Commissioner was learning the ways of the country he had to make way for some one else, who came to Kooloo just as ignorant of the customs and language of the people as was he himself on first arrival. The Assistant, therefore, invested as he is with powers of appeal from all the lower courts in Kooloo, would ordinarily, as a magistrate on the criminal side, be enabled to sentence up to two years' rigorous imprisonment, with fine, and on the civil side to try all cases up to Rs. 10,000 in value, committing either to the Deputy-Commissioner or the Commissioner such cases as are beyond his competence.

During the present year, *i. e.* from 1st May to 20th October, I have decided eighty-five criminal cases and fourteen civil cases, with twenty-seven appeals. The reasons for the dissimilarity in the above proportions will be explained presently, under the head of Crime and Litigation. In addition to his court work, the Assistant-Commissioner has to devote no small portion of his time to the consideration of the many interesting questions concerning trade, customs of the people, and internal organization, which must so frequently arise in such a large extent of country. He is supposed, during his tour of office, to visit every part of his subdivision; and to enable him to do this he must be more on the move than is usual in the plains.

The officials under the Assistant-Commissioner are the Tehsildar of Kooloo, whose head-quarters are at Sooltanpore; the Naib Tehsildar of Plach, who resides at Plach, in Seoraj; the Negee of Lahoul; and the Nono of Spiti.

The Tehsildar of Kooloo has usually the powers of a subordinate magistrate of the first class, and can in criminal cases sentence up to six months' rigorous imprisonment, with fine, and pass orders in civil cases up to Rs. 300.

The Naib Tehsildar of Plach can sentence in criminal cases up to one month's rigorous imprisonment, with fine, and take cognizance of civil suits up to Rs. 50 in value.

The Negee of Lahoul is an honorary magistrate, whose jurisdiction only extends throughout Lahoul, and who is vested *ex officio* with the powers of a subordinate magistrate of the second class, and can therefore imprison up to one month, with fine, and entertain civil suits of the value of Rs. 50.

The Nono of Spiti is also an honorary magistrate; but he has no civil powers, and can only fine up to Rs. 10 on the criminal side.

There is but little work for either of these two last officials. Tara Chund, the Negee of Lahoul, is allowed Rs. 25 *per mensem* for office establishment, and appears, as far as I can judge, to do the duties that fall to his share in a satisfactory manner. The Nono of Spiti, Tanzinnamgyal, is not much burdened by his honorary labours, and is but seldom called upon to exercise the very limited powers he enjoys.

There are police thannahs at Sooltanpore and Plach, each with their complements of deputy-inspectors, sergeants, and constables. The duties demanded of the police are not heavy, and in Seoraj they may be deemed exceedingly light; but as a political measure, it may not be altogether unwise, in a country and among a people who never see a British soldier, European or native, to keep up the police force to its present strength. The principal work the police have to perform is the escorting treasure to Kangra, and guarding prisoners sent there from the sub-division, as all offenders sentenced to above three months' imprisonment have to be forwarded to Dhurmsala jail.

The lock-up in Kooloo is in the Sooltanpore tehseel, which is also the seat of the thannah. At Plach there is likewise a lock-up. Both of these buildings are kept in good order; but I am of opinion that more accommodation should be afforded for prisoners, who might be kept in Kooloo if their sentences were not above six months, as the constant despatch of these men to Kangra weakens the police force very much. It is, besides, an aggravation of the minor punishment to send hill-men to Dhurmsala jail, where the greater heat is regarded with a terror that would be inexplicable were not the results often serious.

The present representative of the ancient kings of Kooloo is Rae Dhuleep Sing, who owns the jaghire of Wuzeeri-Rupi, nominally worth £12,000 per annum, but in reality the annual receipts of this jaghirdar are under £7,000. The last regnant chief of Kooloo was Jeet Sing, who was driven from his throne by the Sikhs in 1840; and at his demise, a distant cousin, by name Thakoor Sing, was presented by Maharajah Shere Sing with the jaghire * that his grandson, the present incumbent, now holds. The title of Rajah was allowed to Thakoor Sing, and the rank of Rae was assumed, with consent of the British Government, by his successor Gyan Sing; but the Kooloo people consider the head of the house as their Rajah; and I do not know but that it would be an act of liberal policy to restore to the present Rae,

* Estate held on a species of feudal tenure.

who is the direct descendant of a long line of kings, the appellation which his ancestral tree would seem to demand. Rae Dhuleep Sing is a minor, and only succeeded his father, Gyan Sing, in August of this year.

Tara Chund, the Negee of Lahoul, was placed in the position of head-man of Lahoul by the British Government, on the previous Negee, Bullee Ram, declining to fill the post. He has been invested, as before mentioned, with both criminal and civil powers, and holds a jaghire worth Rs. 550 per annum; but this is only an appanage of his office, which is, however, hereditary.

Besides Tara Chund, the Negee, there are three other Thakoors in Lahoul, by name Davee Chund, Heera Chund, and Bullee Ram, who all hold considerable tracts of land in jaghire.

When Mr. Egerton, Deputy-Commissioner of Kangra, visited Spiti in 1863, two residents of the Peen valley claimed to be independent of the Nono. One of these individuals, still called the Chota Nono, is descended from Thibetan ancestors, who were professors of medicine, and were granted certain lands in Peen rent free, in lieu of fees. The other claimant for independence was one Chiring, a descendant of those who held the office of Garpon, and this title is still ascribed to him. Apparently there were in Spiti before our rule two head officials, the Nono or Financial Minister, who had the sole control of all fiscal arrangements; and the Garpon, the head military and civil authority; the two being employed to check each other. The individual under notice seems to have held a patent, signed by the Wuzeer of Leh, and sealed with the red seal, which, addressed to one of his ancestors, guaranteed the office of Garpon to the then holder and his successors. Mr. Egerton quashed the claims of both parties, for valid reasons; but it might not be inadvisable, in case of the present Nono ever giving dissatisfaction, to hold the pseudo-Garpon *in terrorem* over him. The Nono Tanzinnamgyal succeeded his father in 1865; he is a well-meaning but very ignorant man, and has but little influence over the Spiti people; he is also unacquainted with any language but Thibetan.

The whole of the subdivision is divided off into *kothees*. Of these there are seventeen in the Upper Beas valley, six in Wuzeeri-Rupi, twenty-seven in Seoraj, thirteen in Lahoul, and five in Spiti. At times there have been more; and, again, one *kothee* has been merged in another; but at present the number is sixty-eight. They follow no particular boundary-lines, but, as a general rule, are comprised in compact limits; but while some contain numerous villages, and afford a considerable return in the way of percentage to the *Negee*, or head-man, others are sparsely populated, and the incomings are almost nominal.

Each *kothee* in Kooloo proper, Wuzeeri-Rupi, and Seoraj has its *Negee*, assisted by a staff of *Lumberdars* and village watchmen, styled *Kronks*. The *Negee*, as he has not only one village, but, in many cases, a considerable number of these under him, is a more important personage than is the *Lumberdar* of the plains; for he is responsible for the revenue from his entire circuit, being remunerated by a small percentage on the collections. It is also the *Negee* who superintends all the arrangements for *begar*, or forced labour, and who is expected to see to the procural of supplies for travellers, the carriage of their baggage, and any demands made by the civil officer on his people for government works. On the whole, he may be regarded as an important functionary; and it mainly depends upon himself whether he is looked up to or not by the men of his *kothee*. Most of the *Negees* can read and write in their own vernacular, but they are, almost without exception, very ignorant, and few have ever been out of Kooloo.

In Lahoul, Tara Chund is the only *Negee*, and in Spiti there are no officials who bear this title, the *Nono* here taking the place the *Negee* occupies in Lahoul, being assisted by five *Gyatpos*, who act in Spiti as do the *Lumberdars* in Kooloo and Lahoul.

The *Lumberdars* in Kooloo and Lahoul, although in a somewhat superior position to the rest of the people in their *kothees*, being excused all *begar*, and receiving, in addition, a tithe for seeing to the collection of revenue, are yet not to be compared to their congeners in the plains. Generally each *kothee*, being divided off into two or more *phuttees*, to every one of these a *Lumberdar* is assigned; and, in the selection of these officials, the wishes of the majority are consulted as far as may be fitting, though, as in the case of the *Negees*, the dignity is hereditary, unless there arise special causes to a contrary ruling.

To each *Lumberdar* is entrusted the carrying out of all demands for *begar* and supplies that have to be furnished by his separate *phuttee;* though any negligence on his part can never be held to excuse the *Negee*, who is primarily responsible for the due performance of duty from all under him; and, on a *Negee's* showing good cause, and proving clearly that one of his *Lumberdars* neglects to obey his orders, and is otherwise contumacious, it has always been my habit to recommend the dismissal of the offender.

The *Lumberdars* in Spiti are attached to each village, just as they are in the plains. They are next in rank to the *Gyatpos*, and carry out their orders; they are also excused from *begar.*

A *Chowkeydar* or *Kronk* is appointed to each *kothee*, and, where the latter is of some size, more than one of these officials becomes necessary. The duties of the *Kronk* are, to some extent, similar to those performed by the village watchmen in the Punjab, but his beat is far more extensive; the post is regarded with favour, and is hereditary. The *Kronk* receives for his services from his *kothee* either a money allowance or regular supplies of grain, and, when he does his work well, he is a very useful official.

The *Putwarries* are, as in the Punjab, the village accountants. Their duty is to register all deeds of sale and transfers of lands, and to keep in proper order the maps and plans of the various *kothees* under their charge, and they occasionally act as registrars of betrothals, &c.

A system has been in force for some years in Kooloo, whereby all betrothals and marriages are, or ought to be, registered. This subject will be alluded to more at length separately; suffice it to say here, that for the carrying on of this work *Punches* * are appointed, who enter in a regular register the dates of betrothal and marriage between contracting parties. The post of Registrar is sought after, and is frequently held by the *Negee* if he can read and write; a small fee is paid for all registrations of the above nature.

From the graver descriptions of crime Kooloo is happily exempt. It is but seldom that serious offences are even brought to the notice of the authorities, and although cases

* In ancient native communities a board of arbitrators usually consisted of five men; and the term *Pānch*, the Oordoo for five, was applied to the entire body. The corrupt Anglo-Indian plural for *Pānch*, *i. e.* Punches, is here employed as it is in very general use.

of theft now and then occur at Sooltanpore, where the population is almost entirely foreign, it may be deemed that the people of the country are singularly free from the majority of the vices that are common elsewhere. Not long ago there were several complaints made by traders, both in Lahoul and Kooloo, of their bales having been ripped open and goods extracted, and it was at one time intended to locate a police force at the foot of the Rohtung Pass, so as to act as a check on these thievish proclivities. A case of this sort came before me in the beginning of 1869, and all implicated were severely punished, notice of the same being sent to every *kothee* in Lahoul and Kooloo, and since then I have not had a charge of this nature brought before me. Assaults occur, but they are nearly always of such a trifling nature that the maxim, *de minimis non curat lex*, may be said to apply to the majority of such suits, and no instance of "grievous hurt" has been ever the cause of inquiry.

The one great blot on the social system

in Kooloo—I refer here more particularly to Kooloo proper—are the customs regulating marriage and betrothal, concerning which fuller information will be found under a separate heading (*vide* Chap. XII.). The faulty action of these customs results in numerous suits for enticing away of women and maintenance of wives; and, till a special enactment is passed which may control the vicious propensities of the people in this respect, I despair of seeing anything approaching to reform.

The civil cases are, as a rule, insignificant, both as to their number and the sums sued for; the people are not litigiously inclined, nor are they very desirous of contesting claims which can be equally well disposed of in a collection of the brotherhood. I have had very few civil cases in my own court. Last year there were several suits before me which concerned sales of opium and mortgages on this class of article, and there were many intricacies in the questions raised, which necessitated a very careful and painstaking series of inquiries. In none of these cases were Kooloo people concerned either as plaintiffs or defendants. This year I have had two curious suits laid in my court. The plaintiff in one sued the defendant (both being Lahoulees) for a considerable sum of money; the plea was that the plaintiff could not claim on the defendant, as the latter was the plaintiff's father, a fact denied by the plaintiff. In the other case, a father sued his son for selling his sheep, the defendant denying the claim, and pleading he had no property separate from his paternal relative. In neither of these suits was it possible to get the parties to come to an understanding, the plaintiffs being fully determined to see the dispute out to its "bitter end." I am satisfied that it is an eminently proper proceeding to invest the Assistant-Commissioner with appellate powers, as the majority of the appeals brought before me, and which, had the Assistant-Commissioner not had the power of hearing, could never have been appealed at all, have shown that the subordinate native officials are by no means to be trusted with too much authority; but here I would specially exempt the present Tehsildar of Kooloo, Khan Chund, from coming within the scope of these remarks, which apply, however, to all others who have served in the subdivision under me, either as Tehsildars or Naib Tehsildars.

Tho supposed custom has been for all native officials in Kooloo to be relieved every two years; but this has been seldom acted up to; some Tehsildars have been kept here for years, while others have been removed after a few months. I cannot refrain from an expression of opinion that these frequent changes are a mistake. The native of the Punjab dislikes Kooloo much, and regards his deputation to the country as a species of exile, and I think it would be right to lay down as a guiding principle, that while two years shall be the very least tenure of office, it should never so happen that the new Assistant-Commissioner and the new Tehsildar enter on office together, as the experience of the one ought always to be utilized to check the ignorance of the other. But while insisting on the Tehsildars remaining for a lengthened period in the valley, I would point out that, separated as this official is from his own countrymen, it is highly desirable to make him contented with his position; with the small pay he at present receives, this is, however, an impossibility. Kooloo is an exceptional country, and those who work for Government in it should be treated in an exceptional manner; the Tehsildar might, with propriety, be invested, *ex officio*, with "full powers" and the full pay of a Tehsildar; while the Naib, at Plach, should have the powers of a subordinate magistrate of the first class. Both these officials should also be encouraged to move about on circuit through their extensive circles, by the receipt of a moderate travelling allowance. The English Assistant-Commissioner approves of Kooloo, with its freedom from severe toil at the desk and its pleasant climate; but his native subordinates look with disgust at their banishment to a country where their compatriots are few, and the little pleasures and accessories to enjoyment which are so essential to a native, can hardly be said to have any existence. The urging of the above points, on my part, is not prompted by a mere good-natured philanthropy, which finds it easy to suggest expenditure that falls on others, but from an innate conviction that the improvements in the prospects of the native officials in Kooloo is essential to the well-being of the interests committed to their charge, and the consequent benefit of the State.

All the Chuprassies * and Messengers (*Muzkoories*) in the tehseels, and, with the Assistant-Commissioner, are natives of the Punjab, nor perhaps has the time yet come for men from Kooloo to take their places. Yet it is only right that the Kooloo people should benefit somewhat by our rule; and selections for the post of Chuprassie might

* A Chuprassie is a species of orderly.

appropriately be made from those who may show, by their intelligence, that they are fitted for Government employment. Education is spreading, though slowly, and it would be quite possible even now to nominate Kooloo men to vacancies that may occur. These appointments are always made from Kangra, but it would be well to reserve a few of such posts for the gift of the Assistant-Commissioner. In time, I trust the judicial establishment may be able to rely on its Kooloo complement; and certainly it would be very pleasing to the inhabitants of the valley, could one of their Negees be granted the post of Naib Tehsildar at Plach; a scheme which I have had the pleasure of discussing with the Rev. Mr. Carleton, when in Seoraj, this season; and one which that gentleman, with many years' experience of the country, stated would have the best possible effect. The individuals, in my opinion, best fitted for such a preferment, are Manohur Negee, of Plach, and Toolsoo Negee, of Chini.

## CHAPTER V.

Earlier History of Kooloo, Lahoul, and Spiti, with some Account of the Inhabitants of each Valley. —Language and Physiognomy of the Natives.— Clothing of Men and Women.—Aspect of the Villages and Houses of the Peasantry.

WHEN the district now known as Kooloo (exclusive of Lahoul and Spiti) was first inhabited, it would be hard to determine, for there are no reliable data which might serve as a guide to the chronologist. I have, however, gone into the subject as thoroughly as I could, and the result of my researches is as follows:—From legendary accounts it is to be gathered that the great Purus Ram, whose valorous deeds have been fully eulogized in Valmeeki's epic, resided in Kooloo for some time, founding the temple at Nirmand, in Seoraj; where he is still worshipped. Marshman places his era at about 1200 B.C.;

but as Purus Ram seems to have lived at a date anterior to the celebrated Yudisthira, who, according to Cunningham, made Indraput (the present Purana Keela, near Delhi) his capital, about B.C. 1430, it appears we must go further back than Marshman would sanction. The idle fables of Hindoo mythology can, of course, find no favour with the educated mind; but it is not improbable that in all these wild stories there may be some admixture of truth; and the tale of Purus Ram's doings at Nirmand, as now repeated in Kooloo, may not, therefore, be altogether without interest.

Purus Ram was one of eight sons of Jumduggun and his wife Ranka. The latter went to see her sister, who was married to King Saharsubahu, and being well treated, she informed her husband of all that had passed. Jumduggun then determined to repay this hospitality, and King Saharsubahu accepted his invitation, and was received with all fitting honour. Jumduggun having in his possession a cow which always gave milk, besides other curiosities, his guest was desirous that the animal should be produced, but the owner positively refused to accede to this request; upon which Saharsubahu endeavoured to force his way into the cattle-shed, and the cow, in poetic phrase, flew up to the sky, or, in plain prose, we may suppose, ran away; but the irate king, drawing his bow, let fly an arrow, which pierced the cow's foot; and hence, says the legend, all cattle have been cloven-footed ever since. Not satisfied with wounding the cow, Saharsubahu now turned on Jumduggun, and either killed or severely maltreated him. At this time Purus Ram was absent, and on his return, his mother Ranka urged him to use his divine power (it will be remembered that this chief is supposed to be an incarnation of Vishnoo in the form of a Brahmin), and restore Jumduggun to life; which was no sooner an accomplished fact, than the resuscitated sufferer instantly ordered Purus Ram to cut off Ranka's head, as she had been the cause of all the late troubles. The son obeyed, and having disposed of his mother, immediately went after his father's enemy, and cut off all Saharsubahu's arms except four, and the latter's name was thenceforth changed to Nag Urjun.

Subsequently Purus Ram engaged in his notorious conflict with the Kshitryas, or warrior race, and having nearly exterminated them, returned to see his father Jumduggun, who, being pleased with his late acts, offered him anything he liked to ask for; on which the dutiful son demanded his mother Ranka's restoration to life, which request was at once granted. But Purus Ram, as the slayer of his mother, was not held in favour by his brethren; and in expiation of his offences, he gave various lands to Brahmins; as, for instance, five villages on the Nerbudda, five on the Sutledj, and four on the Beas. The villages on the Sutledj were Kao, Mael, Nuggur, Nirt, and Nirmand, and the donor fixed the limits of the jaghires, and gave the holders leases on copper sheets, which, to this day, the Nirmand priests declare are to be seen in their temple! He also gave the Nirmand Brahmins a figure of the goddess Ambka to worship; and instituted tri-yearly feasts or festivals, which have been kept up ever since.

How much of fable there is in the above it would be hard to say; but if Purus Ram be a true personage, and really did give these villages to the priests, we may suppose Kooloo can be held to have been inhabited in the fifteenth century B.C. I must now take up the story of another series of personages, who seem to have lived about Purus Ram's time.

A chief, or, as the people call him, a demon, by name Tandee, fixed his abode on the Kooloo side of the Rohtung Pass, and with him lived his sister Hurimba, whose temple is now at Doongree, near Menalee, in the Upper Beas valley. Bhaem Sen, the Pandu, next appears on the scene, his mission being to clear Kooloo of all the demons in it; but in this instance he contented himself with running off with Hurimba, and Tandee, aggrieved at this, fought with Bhaem Sen, and was in the conflict slain. With Bhaem Sen was a follower, one Bidher, who however was not a Pandu, and this man married a daughter of Tandee's. Two sons were the fruit of this union, one called Bhot, and the other Mukhur, both these boys being brought up by the goddess Beas Ricki. Bhot married a woman named Soodungee, who came from Bhotunt, and this marriage seems to have been attended with unfortunate results, for Soodungee, with no fear of the Brahmins before her eyes, cooked cow's flesh one day, and gave this to Bhot. Mukhur was not present during this act of impiety, and when he came in, Beas Ricki told him what had occurred; upon which Mukhur, who had apparently been indoctrinated with strictly Brahminical principles, fled to a spot somewhere to the south of Sooltanpore, and there founded a village called Mukraha, and Kooloo after him obtained the name of Mukarsa, by which it was known till a recent period. The old capital of the Rajahs, at Nuggur, was termed Mukarsa; and Moorcroft, when in Kooloo, in 1819, mentions that he passed below the site of this ancient city. The territory of Kooloo was considered the last boundaries of civilization by the Hindoos; and the cognomen of Koolunt Peeth (the end of the inhabited world) was conferred on it, the change to Kooloo occurring in the lapse of years. About the time of Purus Ram and Mukhur, it seems that there were many petty chiefs both in Seoraj and the Upper Beas valley, for it is stated Purus Ram's brother (?), Behungamunnee came to Manikurn, in the Parbuttee valley, even then a noted shrine, and seized some territory close by; but being driven out, he took refuge at Juggutsookh, and after some vicissitudes of fortune, succeeded in conquering a considerable portion of the Upper Beas valley.

From this Behungamunnee descended, according to native tradition, no less than seventy-seven Pals, the last being Sidh Pal, who, it is said, reigned from A.D. 1321 to

1357,* and who dropped the title of Pal, and took that of Rajah, henceforth adopted by his successors, of whom there were fourteen up to Jeet Sing, the last reigning sovereign in Kooloo, who was ousted from his throne by the Sikhs in 1840.

The actual descendants of Behungamunnee, who would, in the ordinary course, have succeeded him had there not been interregnums, were eighty-five, which, with the fifteen rajahs, allowing an average reign, or what answers to a reign, to each of fifteen years, gives us 100 chiefs, who in all ruled 1,500 years. Now Jeet Sing lost his life in 1840, which would give the date of Behungamunnee's advent to a chieftainship in Kooloo at A.D. 310. Here there is clearly some error, for this ruler and Purus Ram were, it is stated, brothers; so it must either be that Purus Ram's era is long antecedent to Behungamunnee's, as Purus Ram lived in the fifteenth century before Christ, or,

* This date is not to be in the very least relied on.

that the names of more than half the Pals who reigned have been altogether lost sight of. The native chronicles state that the goddess Hurimba appeared to Behungamunnee, and promised him the chieftainship of Kooloo; but it was before affirmed that Hurimba and Purus Ram lived at the same time; so it may be gathered that the Behungamunnee given as the first Pal of Kooloo, was not brother to Purus Ram, and actually lived at a much later period; and this seems the more natural supposition.

Allowing, however, that the genealogical roll of Pals is correct, it is to be gathered that, up to the reign of Ootum Pal, the capital of the chiefs was at Nast or Juggut-sookh, in the Upper Beas valley; when it was transferred to Nuggur, called also Mukarsa. At this time, and for many years after, the only territory held by the Pals of Kooloo was that portion which lies between Sooltanpore and the Rohtung Pass, and it was not until the reign of Bahadur Sing (about 1400 A.D.?) that Wuzeeri-Rupi and

Seoraj were annexed. In Juggut Sing's reign (1660 A.D.) the capital was transferred to Sooltanpore from Nuggur, the name Sooltanpore being given to it, from one Sooltan Chund, the brother of a minor chief, from whom it had been wrested. After this the kingdom was much enlarged, till, in the reign of Rajah Maun Sing (in the latter part of the 18th century probably) the boundaries of the state enclosed a very considerable area of country, which extended nearly up to Simla on one side, and to the town of Mundee on the other; Lahoul, Bara Banghal, and Spiti being also under this chief's sway, the whole of whose dominions must have comprised at least 10,000 square miles. The advent of the Sikhs coming soon after internal troubles, which had much reduced the importance of what had doubtless been once a great state, soon effected the long-impending ruin; and on Jeet Sing's defeat and death, in 1840, the Sikhs selected a distant cousin of the late sovereign as his successor, but only conferred on him the jaghire of Wuzeeri-Rupi, now held by his descendant, Rae Dhuleep Sing. Lamentably deficient as the records in the hands of the family priests (*perohits*) are in the matter of dates, yet every now and then clues are given as to the periods in which events occurred, that might, with a little research, afford an insight into the eras of the various chiefs. In the rule of Shureedut Taeshur, the 31st Pal, it is mentioned that Umr Sing ruled in Chumba, and Goburdun at Indraprust, *i. e.* Delhi; but I have been unable to fix the dates of the reigns of these sovereigns. The 50th Pal, Sichundur, it appears, paid a visit to the Delhi Rajah, with entreaties for aid, as the Chinese (?) had invaded Kooloo; and it is asserted that the Delhi army marched through Kooloo, and seized part of Baltistan, Roopshoo, and the country as far as the lake Mantilae. This is a curious record, and still more curious if true, and it has an aspect of veracity about it, as the lake, now called Manasorowa, was in old days termed Mantilae, and it would be interesting to ascertain whether Indian armies had ever successfully penetrated so far north as this. In the reign of the 54th Pal, Ali Shere Khan governed Cashmere, and, in the reign of the 56th Pal, Kooloo fell under the sway of Bussahir. When the 62nd chief, Nund Pal, ruled, Kooloo was taken possession of by a Kangra army, and in Keral Pal's time, he being the 67th from Behungamunnee, the Rajah of Sookhet occupied nearly the entire country. I have seen in the possession of Heera Sing (a cousin of the present Rae's) a series of original letters addressed by Shah Jehan, Dara Sheko, and Aurungzib to Rajah Juggut Sing, termed by them *Zemindar* of Kooloo. These fix the date of this chief's reign between the years 1640 and 1680 A.D., but he is almost the only sovereign of the country whose era I have been able to gather with any approach to exactitude.

I propose to write a separate account of the history of Kooloo, the materials for which I have at hand, but the few facts given above may, perhaps, not be deemed out of place here.

It is not probable that the population of either Seoraj, Wuzeeri-Rupi, or Kooloo proper has changed much in its style of inhabitants of late years. There may have been emigration from Mundee and Bunghal, and it is known that, in the reign of Rajah Juggut Sing, Hindoos in large numbers came up from the plains; but these accessions could have but little affected the masses of the existing population. Many Kangra shopkeepers have settled in the valley, and merchants from even Umballah and Umritsur have stores at Sooltanpore.

The population throughout Kooloo may be said to consist almost entirely of *Kaneits* and *Daghees*, with a slight infusion of *Brahmins*, a large proportion of the rent-free lands being in the hands of the latter.

The *Brahmins*, with very few exceptions, cultivate their own lands, but the *Kaneits* are the largest landowners, their tenure being, in olden times, a species of feudatory one, which involved personal service in the field. The *Daghees* are also *Zemindars*, though this last term is never applied to them in Kooloo; their holdings, as a rule, are much smaller than those of the *Kaneits*.

The *Brahmins* and *Rajpoots* are not numerous, and differ hardly at all from the *Kaneits* in either dress or appearance. Some of the leading *Brahmins* wear small gold earrings, and their women have not the small round cap commonly in use with the females of other castes.

The *Sunyars* or goldsmiths, who are said to have come from the plains of late years, commonly, as do the *Brahmins*, marry *Kaneit* girls, known as *Staet*, in distinction to the *Lari*, or wife of the same caste taken in regular marriage. Mr. Lyall mentions, in his census report of Kooloo, that the children of a *Kaneit* wife by a Brahmin are called *Brahmins* or *Rajpoots*, the term *Ratee* being often added as a qualification by the *Lari* wife in the presence of other children.

The Kooloo *Kaneits* are sometimes supposed to be the same as the *Ratees* of Kangra, who have lost caste by taking to the plough. The two classes are called *Karsyas* and *Raos*, who intermarry, and will eat together from the same dish; the first call themselves *Rajpoots*, but the *Raos* do not admit their superiority.

The *Tawees* are masons, and rank between *Kaneits* and *Daghees*.

The *Burhaes* are *Daghees*, who work as carpenters, but consider themselves a separate caste. The *Naths*, *Byragees*, and *Goosains*, though in name clerics, are all seculars, and have wives and families. The *Byragees* are supposed to have come from Oudh, in Rajah Juggut Sing's reign, being encouraged to settle to promote the worship of Vishnu, which was not in favour before their arrival; and it is known that a large body of these men entered Kooloo sometime subsequent to this, and were then employed in quelling a revolt. Most of the *Byragees* of the present day are descendants of *Brahmins* and *Kaneits*. The *Naths* are *Daghees*, and have now no pretensions to a religious character: they are recognizable by the enormous wooden earrings they wear.

The musicians in Kooloo numbered 2,414 in the census of 1868; they are nearly all *Daghees*, holding small plots of land from the temple grants, in consideration of the usual service of drum-beating, horn-blowing, and pipe-playing.

The *Daghees* are also termed *Bugaroo* or *Kolees*, the latter name being given to all Kooloo people by those from the plains. In Seoraj the *Daghees* are frequently called *Breetoos;* but should any of them take to trade, they are designated after their special avocations; such as *Bewarees*, basket-makers; *Barhies*, carpenters; *Dunganees*, iron-smelters; *Poombees*, wool-cleaners, &c.; and these appellations adhere to families who have quite abandoned such trades.

Even in the lowest caste of *Daghee* there are subdivisions, and *Chumars* and *Lohars* form themselves into brotherhoods, but many *Daghees* refuse to intermarry with those who call themselves either *Lohars* or *Chumars*. The *Daghee* will eat the flesh of animals that have died a natural death, but the *Lohars* are said to be more particular. The *Daghees* may be held to stand in a sort of subordinate rank to the *Kaneits*, though there is often nothing in their appearance that would lead an indifferent observer to notice that the two were of different castes. Mr. Lyall mentions that the *Daghees* "are said to be *Koreedars*, or courtyard wallahs of certain *Kaneit* families or villages. When a *Kaneit* dies, his heirs call the *Jutai* or head-man of their *Koreedar Daghees*: these last bring in wood for the funeral pile and for the wake or funeral feast, and torches; play the pipes and drums in the funeral procession, and do other services, in return for which they get food and the *kiria*, or funeral perquisites."

The population of Kooloo proper in the census of 1868 amounted to 33,410; of Wuzeeri-Rupi, to 12,496; and of Seoraj, to 44,355.

The earlier history of Lahoul can only be

gathered from old traditions, as any written records do not apparently exist. Before Lahoul came under the sway of the Rajahs of Kooloo, it was one of the provinces of the petty Buddhist kingdom of Gugè, which borders Chumurti and Upper Kunawur, and it is stated that the Gyalpos of Ladakh never ruled in the valley at all. When attached to Gugè, which is in Thibet proper, Lahoul was larger than it is now, both Triloknath and Pangi, at present in Chumba territory, having been within its limits. About the time of Boodhee Sing or Maun Sing, rajahs of Kooloo in the latter end of the seventeenth or beginning of the eighteenth century, the Gugè Government in Lahoul had become almost powerless; and the Chumba Rajah, taking advantage of this state of affairs, acquired considerable influence in Lahoul; more particularly was this influence felt towards Pangi and Triloknath, and for many years a nominal tribute was regularly demanded, a part of which consisted of twelve large dogs; and at the same time the leading men in

Chumba were accustomed to levy certain dues on their own account; such as woollen cloth, ropes, &c. &c. Rajah Boodhee Sing, of Kooloo, married a daughter of the ruler of Kishtwar, and he himself went to that country to bring his bride home, *viâ* Lahoul, and he is said to have taken the opportunity *en route* of impressing on the Lahoulees the advisability of throwing off the yoke of Gugè, and of giving their allegiance to the Kooloo state. Lahoul was then, it seems, annexed to Kooloo; and it is said Rajah Boodhee Sing introduced various improvements in the administration; among which was the chief one of paying the revenue in cash instead of in kind. There can be little doubt but that both Chumba and Kooloo were, at this period, in accord as to the wresting of Lahoul from Gugè; and Boodhee Sing being satisfied with that part of the country now under British rule, the remainder, that lay in what is now known as Chumba territory, was seized by the Rajah of the latter principality. Gugè never attempted to interfere with this act of spoliation, and, until the reign of Jeet Sing, almost the whole of Lahoul was in the possession of the Kooloo chiefs; when, on this Rajah's expulsion from his kingdom, in 1840, it reverted to the Sikhs, and again to the British in 1846.

There was, according to popular accounts, an invasion of Lahoul by the Mongols, under a leader named Goldan Tsewang, some 180 years ago; these people were Buddhists, and it is affirmed that they remained in the conquered territory for a year or two, this being while Lahoul was still under Gugè. The Rev. Mr. Heyde,* who has in the most obliging manner placed all the above information at my disposal, has mentioned to me that in different localities in Lahoul, old tombs have been found by the *Zemindars*, when ploughing or digging foundations for buildings. Now, as the Buddhists do not bury their

* This gentleman is one of the Moravian missionaries at Kielung, in Lahoul.

dead in graves, it is extremely probable that there was an invasion of Lahoul by some Mahomedan power, probably in the time of Genghis Khan; and the traditions in Lahoul point to a people beyond Yarkund as the builders of these tombs. Ten years is assigned as the period during which these northern hordes remained in the valley, during which time the Lahoulees took refuge in the upper heights, and there cultivated and resided. When this incursion of the Mahomedans occurred, it is not known who governed Lahoul, but it is confidently stated that the invasion was anterior to the subjection of the country by Gugè.

Within the last sixty or seventy years there has been a considerable emigration into Lahoul from Bara Banghal, Chumba, Zanskar, and other parts of Ladakh.

In Lahoul, at the census of 1868, there were 216 *Brahmins*, 502 *Kaneits*, 4,566 *Daghees*, 277 *Burrarars*, 10 Sawyers, and 3 *Hensees*, besides other miscellaneous castes. The *Thakoors* are the jaghirdars, or their offshoots; and these, although of purely Thibetan blood, are beginning to assert a *Rajpoot* origin. The *Brahmins* are only found in *Puttun*, the valley of the Chundra Bagha, and are emigrants from Chumba, or other countries. The *Kaneits* are partly Thibetan and partly true *Kaneits*. It is supposed that the majority of the inhabitants of *Puttun* are descendants of settlers from Kooloo or Banghal; the people elsewhere being pure Thibetans, and, with the exception of the *Brahmins*, all are Buddhists; but the Lahoulees are so much thrown into contact with the Kooloo people, that they are gradually becoming Hinduised. The *Daghees* are said to have come from Kooloo; and, as in the latter district, they are also in Lahoul the menial caste, and are bound to give service as porters, and provide firewood, &c., at encamping-grounds. They also act as musicians in the monasteries and temples. The *Lohars*, or blacksmiths, are a caste of about the same standing as the *Daghees*, if, indeed, they are not *Daghees;* the *Burrarars* weave blankets, and the *Hensees* are professional musicians, their wives and daughters performing as nautch-girls. The population of Lahoul, in the census of 1868, amounted to 6,265 souls.

Mr. Egerton, in his most interesting "Journal of a Tour through Spiti," collated all the information obtainable regarding the earlier history of this valley; and I cannot do better than refer to his statements, which will, however, be here a good deal summarized. The earliest reliable notice we have of Spiti occurs about the year 1055 A.D., when the country was apparently under the rule of Thibet, of which Lhassa was the seat of government; and when Thibet fell, in 1262, under the sway of the emperor Kublae Khan, "Spiti probably shared the same fate." Cosmos de Koros alludes to the foundation of the Rareng or Kee monastery in the middle of the eleventh century by the pupil of Pundit Atisha, who is better known in Kunawur *

* A district of Bussahir, adjoining Spiti.

by his other name of Choro, and who, we are told, proceeded to Lhassa on quitting Hindostan. When the Tartar empire disappeared, Spiti, it seems, remained as a feudatory to Chinese Thibet; but by the commencement of the seventeenth century it came under the rule of the Buddhist *Gyalpo* Jamya of Ladakh. On the defeat of this chief by Ali Meer, of Balti, Spiti, with other outlying provinces, revolted, and became partially independent; until, at Jamya's death, his son Singge Namgyal overcame the Baltis about A.D. 1635, and reconquered Spiti. The territory of Singge, on his demise, being divided among his three sons, Deldan, Indra, and Tenchog, the latter obtained possession of Zanskar and Spiti, this division taking place between 1660 and 1670. About 1710 Delek, the son of Deldan, *Gyalpo* of Ladakh, warred against Gugè, which state called in the aid of the Lhassan army; and this interference ended in the annexation of both Gugè and Spiti by the Lhassans, for, in A.D. 1720, Delek made peace with the latter, and, marrying the daughter of the Lhassan general, received with her Spiti as his dowry. In 1740, or thereabouts, the Baltis again conquered Ladakh, and perhaps Spiti was once more held for a time by the Balti chief; but if this occupation ever occurred, it could only have been for a short time. When Runjeet Sing seized Cashmere, he exacted tribute from Ladakh, and Spiti at that period paid revenue to the latter, besides a *nuzzurana* * to the Rajahs of Kooloo and Bussahir. In 1841, Zorawur Sing, the general of Rajah Gholab Sing, of Cashmere, invaded Ladakh, and placed one Ruheem Khan in charge of Spiti; and Gholam Khan, the son-in-law of this man, employed himself with the plundering of the monasteries in the valley. In December of the same year, Zorawur Sing's forces were entirely destroyed by the Lhassans in the lofty plains near the Rawan Hrad lake, above the course of the Sutledj; and then the Spiti people turned on their oppressor, and slew him. In 1842 the Lhassan armies invaded Ladakh, but they

* A species of tribute.

were eventually expelled, and an arrangement was entered into, whereby all the southern provinces of Ladakh were ceded once more to the Rajah of Cashmere. Spiti fell under this category; but as it was deemed unadvisable to allow a rival territory to stretch between the Sutledj and the shawl-wool districts of Chang-Thang, an exchange was effected, and Spiti was annexed to the British empire. It was farmed out to Mansookh Dass, Wuzeer of Bussahir, for 1846–47–48, and only taken under the direct management of the Assistant-Commissioner of Kooloo in 1849.

It may be a matter of surprise that Spiti, so very poor a country, should ever have been deemed worth the trouble of conquering; and that its inhabitants, who only can be approached by most difficult passes, should have been unable to retain their independence. But it would seem that an invading army had only to appear for the Spiti men to at once submit; and even had they been a warlike race, it would have been difficult, with such a scanty population, to guard all the passes for any length of time; and it must be remembered they were exposed to enemies on all sides, who never dreamt of declaring war, or giving any time for preparation, invading the valley simply because it was their pleasure to do so.

The inhabitants of Spiti are *Bhots*, with a strong infusion of Tartar blood; and it is known that not many years ago, a colony of 200 persons emigrated from what the people call China, but which was, in all probability, the territory of Great Thibet.

In Spiti there are no castes, in the usual acceptation of that term, for all eat and drink together; but *Kaneits* do not marry with *Lohars*, nor the latter with *Bedas*. The *Kaneits* are, in truth, pure Thibetans, and may be said to constitute the majority of the inhabitants, there being only 100 *Lohars* and 46 *Bedas*, the latter answering to the *Hensees*, or musicians of Lahoul, and holding no lands; the saying in Spiti, quoted by Mr. Lyall,* being, "the *Beda* no land, the

* Mr. Lyall was Settlement Officer of the Kangra district when this was written.

dog no load." The *Lohars* are good blacksmiths, and most of them own a little land.

The priestly class will be noticed in a separate chapter.

The population of Spiti, in the census of 1868, amounted to 2,272.

In Kooloo the dialect in common use is made up chiefly of *Sanskrit*, *Oordoo*, and *Paharee*, a *patois* of the hills, with an infusion of Thibetan words, which last become more noticeable in the upper portion of the valley, towards the Rohtung Pass. In the out-of-the-way villages, the people know hardly anything of *Oordoo*, nor can what they say be understood by those who have not some acquaintance with *Paharee*. At the village of Malauna (see also Chap. XIII.) the people have a dialect which is only known to themselves; and here, although the hamlet is far out of reach of contact with the Thibetans of Lahoul or Spiti, situated as it is off the Parbuttee valley, there are many pure Thibetan words in use, and this notwithstanding the fact that Thibetan is quite unknown in any of the surrounding villages.

In Lahoul there are four languages: first, the true Thibetan, generally used about Kolung, in the Bagha valley, and at Koksur, in the Chundra valley; secondly, Boonuun, spoken in Davee Chund's *jaghire* at Goomerung kothee, Kardung *kothee*, and Barbok *kothee*, this dialect being half Thibetan as far as the words go, but a separate language as far as grammar is concerned; thirdly, Mănchăt, or, in vernacular papers, *Puttun*, composed of Hindee principally, a little Thibetan, and the rest quite a local language: this is spoken in the six *kothees* by the Chundra Bagha, viz. at Tandee, Warpa, Ranee-ka, Yanampel or Yampee, Jobrong, and Goee or Gooshall; fourthly, Teenuun, made up with Thibetan words, Mănchăt, Boonuun, a little Hindee, and some few Persian words: this is used in *kothee* Gondla, on the Chundra. For the above information I am indebted to the courtesy of the Rev. Mr. Heyde, Moravian missionary at Kielung, who has devoted some research to the study of the dialects of Lahoul. Nearly all Lahoulees can make themselves intelligible in Oordoo.

The language in Spiti is pure Thibetan, and there are not a dozen people in the country who can speak or understand *Oordoo.*

The inhabitants of Kooloo proper, Wuzeeri-Rupi, and Seoraj partake largely of the distinguishing features of the Hindoos of the plains. The men are, as a rule, of the medium height, and are strongly built, with intelligent and pleasing faces. Except in certain localities, the hair is not worn long, and it is rarely that large beards or whiskers are to be met with. The women, and more particularly those in the Upper Beas valley, whether from the greater variety in their picturesque attire, or whether from a really superior style of feature, are more prepossessing than are the men; and many of the children, when young, are quite beautiful.

The Lahoulees are not a comely race, and the intermixture of Hindoo and Tartar blood has failed in producing a population remarkable for good looks. Both sexes are short, and the women, perhaps, bear off the palm for ugliness, the Mongolian origin of the race being shown, in many cases, by the oblique eyes, flat face, and large mouth; but the Hindoo type is not unfrequently observable, and there are both handsome men and women to be found in Lahoul.

The people of Spiti bear unmistakable evidences on their faces of their Chinese or Mongolian descent. The men are stout, well-built fellows, and the women are also very strongly framed. Many of the men resemble veritable Calmucks; and, with few exceptions, fall, as do the women, very far below the European standard of beauty; indeed, for positive hideousness of countenance, the people of Spiti are, perhaps, pre-eminent in the British empire; but their looks are the worst part about them, as I shall further on hope to show.

There are certain minor varieties of attire throughout Kooloo; but there are, after all, no very great differences worthy of particular comment. The men in summer wear loose grey woollen trousers, and a short coat of the same material, which, as winter comes on, is covered with a country blanket wound round the body, and brought over the shoulders, much as is a Highlander's plaid. The waist is bound with another cloth, either of linen or *puttoo;* and the head-dress consists of a black or deep maroon-coloured cap of rolled cloth, with a patch of red at the top. A species of skull-cap, with a border round the neck and ears, much the same in form as that furnished to Punjab prisoners, is also a good deal affected, and this is occasionally trimmed with an edging of red cloth. In one or two villages in the Surburri valley it is against custom ever to wear trousers. The dress of the Kooloo zemindar, when clean, which it seldom is, is both fitting and decent; and at *melas* or fairs, when every one dons his best, the most fastidious could hardly see room for fault-finding. In the Surburri valley (towards the top of the Bubboo Pass) the men wear the pig-tail, but this is secured under the cap. Ornaments, in the way of jewellery, are not affected by the males; but every well-to-do *Zemindar* wears a silver necklace, with a coin-like pendant, and the higher classes of Brahmins deck themselves with small gold earrings, while some of the richer villagers adorn their wrists with silver bracelets. Towards Seoraj grass shoes are in common use; and in Wuzeeri-Rupi and Kooloo proper the men are either barefooted or have Hindustani shoes. A simple straw shoe, that only lasts a few days, may, however, also be said to be in general adoption.

The body-dress of the women consists of a large plaid, one end of which is brought over the left shoulder, then passed behind the back, under the right arm, across the bosom, and under the left arm, and over the first fold at the back; so that the projecting corner may lie over the right shoulder, the lappets being secured to the main portion of the costume in front by long brass or silver pins, also used by the men, and which pins are connected together by coloured string, or a silver or brass chain. The plaids are of very different colours, from a whitish-grey and deep maroon or brown, to black and white check; but in the former there is always a running pattern of coloured lines, or a border in tiers of different hues; green, however, never appears in their costume. This does not arise from their dislike to the colour, but from inability to procure the dye. I have never yet seen any Kooloo woman with any article of green in her dress; but that they have no objection to the tint is clear, as it is common to see them with green leaves fastened in the hair. Round the waist a smaller blanket is invariably worn; and in the winter woollen trousers are adopted; but in the summer they are, for the most part, bare-legged, though the wives of the richer *Zemindars* may occasionally be observed with cotton trousers, of a nondescript blue-and-red pattern. The female head-dresses in Kooloo are numerous. In the Surburri valley, and in one or two other localities, the women wear the same round caps as do the men; and in a few villages near Nuggur, in the Upper Beas valley, above Manikurn, in the Parbuttee valley, and at Malauna village, it is customary for the females to fling over their heads a curious brown cope, which exactly resembles a friar's hood. Throughout Kooloo generally there are three descriptions of head-dress: the loose kerchief of blue, red, or yellow cotton; the small cap, secured by a fillet or two of bright wool; or the full gala attire. For this last style the procedure is as follows:—the hair is swept off the front, and gathered into a mass behind, and round this are wound several lengths of scarlet wool; the projecting hair is then plaited into the worsted tail, which is of a deep brown colour, and hangs nearly to the ground, ending in a loose tassel. The small cap, of cherry and yellow, or white and brown, in alternate bars, is then coquettishly perched over the forehead, and is fixed on with two or three pieces of bright wool; the long tail is now caught up, and thrown in a couple of folds round the head, the long tassel at the end sweeping carelessly over the entire head-piece. A profusion of silver earrings is worn, the ears being pierced all round the edges to receive them; and the unsightly disfigurement this feature suffers, being cut in so many places, and then forced down by both the weight of ornament and the pressure of the head-dress, is the one false point about the Kooloo idea of beauty, and is too much a part of the habit of the country to be ever set right. Across the brow bands of silver, with jointed pendants, are arranged; and, to complete the picture, there are coral, lapis lazuli, and bead necklaces in numbers, besides a substantial silver bracelet on either arm. Many of the Kooloo women are strikingly handsome, and their very light complexions, rosy lips, brown hair, and sparkling eyes would be noticeable features in any country in the world. *Brahmin* women never wear the cap, nor do unmarried girls of other castes; the hair of the latter being woven into the worsted pig-tail before alluded to.

The dress of the Lahoul *Zemindar* is not very dissimilar to that of the Kooloo peasant, but he prefers a fabric of a darker hue, and discards the waist-cloth and the red patch on the top of the cap.

The hair of the Lahoulee women is twisted in numerous braids, and these are gathered together at the back and fastened either into a scallop-shell, or strung to beads, and, on the crown of the head, that is always bare, a small and rather elegantly-chased saucer of silver is affixed; this is set round in the inside with coral and turquoise, garnished with gold, and occasionally on the forehead a rough specimen of turquoise is secured into the hair. The dress is a long black woollen garment, fastened by a waist-cloth; thick trousers of the same material, and grass shoes completing the attire. Necklaces and earrings of amber and rough stones are also common.

The costume of the men of Spiti is peculiar, and differs *in toto* from that worn either in Kooloo or Lahoul. The body garment of the males is a long loose grey coat, of a very substantial cloth, that is peculiar to Spiti; this is tightened round the waist by a roll of coloured fabric, made up of cotton and silk, and sometimes the arms of the coat are turned back from the wrists, and exhibit a white lining, marked by a wide border of crimson, a fringe of similar hue being bound round the skirts and front of the robe. Trousers of the same substance as the waist-cloth are occasionally worn; but again these are often of coarse silk, streaked horizontally black and white, and, seen as they are just below the coat, they present something of the appearance of stockings. Two descriptions of head-dress are in fashion. One of these is a small round skull-cap, which, when new, is not an unattractive object. The framework of the cap is covered with black cloth, and a broad band of green or red is sewn round the lower part, on either side of which are white pipings, that run up also to the centre, where a small red knot is fixed, and to this are occasionally attached tags of coloured silk, cloth, or thread. The other head-dress is the Ladakh type, and is probably borrowed from that country. A bag of thick furred cloth, like plush, either grey or black, is sewn together, the open end being a trifle larger than the head; this is then one half lined with red or yellow, and the other half with blue or purple. The end is now turned back and fixed on the head, the flap hanging on one side, somewhat in the style of a Highlander's bonnet. Among the wealthier classes these caps are made of beaver-skin outside, and lined with yellow China silk. Over the coat a loose reddish-coloured piece of half-silk, half-wool is carelessly thrown. In the summer the common native shoe is worn by both sexes; and, in winter, a very curious sort of boot, which, although rude of structure, answers admirably for all purposes of warmth and protection. The lower portion of this boot is made of untanned leather, which is worked, when wet, into a rough shape of the foot; to the inside of this is attached another piece of leather, coloured light brown, to cover the ancles and instep, and to this is sewn a coarse blanketing, that comes nearly up to the knee. When this boot (worn by both sexes) is put on, it is seldom taken off for some days, and, for warmth's sake, it is filled with flour, and the blanketing is then tied with a string below the knee. Every Spiti *Zemindar* wears ear-rings of coral and turquoise, with large necklaces of these stones, mixed with glass, crystal, and huge lumps of amber. I have never seen a Spiti man with beard or whiskers, and even tolerably-sized moustachios are rarely met with; it is a common custom also to shave the head, leaving only a pigtail, *à la Chinois*, which hangs down the back. Each *Zemindar* carries his steel pipe, brass strike-light, called a *chukmuk*, and tobacco-pouch; and in the bosom of his coat is to be found the wooden cup used in eating, which, with a sheathed knife, steel penholder stuck in his belt, and a curiously-framed steel key, finish off his attire.

The dress of the women in Spiti is much gayer than that of the men. They wear no caps on their heads, but over each ear is arranged a large flap or lappet of cloth covered with dyed wool, and fastened over the braids of hair; and, from the brow down the back to the waist is adjusted a broad band of red cloth, studded with large turquoises and other stones of very dubious value; this is termed the *perak*. Besides the above, every wife of a well-to-do *Zemindar* has a profusion of earrings, noserings, and necklaces of very solid gold and silver, picked out with beads and stones, and silver and white shell bracelets; showing, in all, an array of ornament which makes most women in Spiti as they stand worth from £12 to £15 in jewellery. The body costume is made up of a dark cloth coat, coming down below the knees, strong trousers of a reddish fibre, and either grass shoes or leather boots.

The *Lamas* are all bareheaded, except on state occasions, when they attire themselves in very curious head-dresses; they wear red or yellow coats, with no trousers. The yellow dress is preferred for cheapness, but each sect of Buddhists has its own appropriate colour, though this, at any rate in Spiti, is not rigidly adhered to.

In an ordinary Kooloo village the houses will be found arranged in a rude disorder, that bears little approach to the semblance of streets; still, there frequently is at least one line of houses, which, if the facilities of the ground permit, is paralleled with another row for some short way, the buildings at either extremity tailing off, and separating more widely from the rest of the hamlet. As a rule, the *Brahmins* take the highest sites, though this is not always observed, the *Kaneits*, the *Daghees*, and the subdivisions of the latter caste occupying the lower tier of houses; but it may be noticed that, adjoining the *Brahmin* quarter, there are often small and not uncomfortable sheds, which have been granted rent-free to some low-caste family, and for this charity no return is looked for; nor are the *Daghees* even expected to help in the fields, or in the household duties of cleansing rice, preparing oil, &c., though it will be generally found the generosity of the *Brahmin* is not lost sight of by those residing on his property.

At all times a Kooloo *Zemindar's* house is a somewhat picturesque object, with its gabled roof of slate or shingle, its overhanging verandahs, and the massive stone walls, surrounded by the flat paved court. In Seoraj and Wuzeeri-Rupi it is not uncommon to build houses three and sometimes four storeys in height, but in Kooloo proper the double storey is preferred; the upper apartments being reserved for the household, and the lower ones applied to the stacking of grain or stalling of cattle. Some of the Kooloo villages are large, and have over a hundred houses; but others, again, are merely detached clusters of a few buildings, which in either case follow, in certain particulars, the architectural details to be found in Switzerland. The walls, occasionally whitewashed or plastered with mud, are formed of tiers of beams and rubble masonry, the timbers for the ceilings of the lower and upper storeys projecting, the first to receive the verandahs, and the second to support the slates of the main roof. The entrance is from below, a rough ladder leading to the household apartments; but, where the verandah is of no great height from the ground, a similar ladder, formed of a log cut in niches, leads direct to the upper rooms. The verandahs may either extend all round the house,—and this they often do, or but on two sides, being closed in to the main roof for the greater part, openings, however, being left here and there by means of carved windows. In the poorer style of dwelling the verandahs are open all round, with now and then a protecting railing between the supports, and it is the fashion, in the loftier houses, to have one or two poles projecting out below the verandahs, across which broad flat planks are loosely placed. Below is the paved enclosure, used for treading the corn, oil-pressing, rice-cleaning, or for spreading out the hay to dry.

A village in the Upper Beas valley is far from an uninteresting study. In the spring the cut corn is to be seen lying loosely about, or dangling in great sheaves from the verandahs, which also are crowded with the overplus of the ricks below; and, as summer changes into autumn, the rich green grass is strewn over each get-at-able roof or flat surface, mixed with the rich yellow Indian corn, which is cast in ruddy layers on every housetop, pleasantly breaking with its refreshing tints the more sombre browns and greys of the adjacent tenements. It is at this season, too, that the pumpkins, with their large golden flowers and enormous leaves of most vivid green, combined with a description of climbing bean and a wild vine, cluster up the rude scantlings, and invade the very verandahs; or, passing in airy bridges along the poles across the roadway, soften off all architectural angularities with their pendent and wide-spreading leaves and tendrils. In the verandahs are to be seen the women with their scarlet, blue, or yellow kerchiefs, attending to their children, or below in the courtyard, assisting to spread out the grass they have just brought in, or in couples, working with a will at the cleaning of the rice from the husk, a process requiring a good deal of toil, a stout pole being forced with considerable energy, as a species of gigantic pestle, into the hollowed stone which contains the grain, the labour being accompanied by a pleasant sort of murmuring song, not unlike that used by sailors when pulling at a rope. In this courtyard, which is generally closed in by a wall of stones, are other holes, in which the oil from the kernels of apricots, peaches, and vegetable herbs is expressed, and it is not unusual to see two or three of the gentler sex pounding away in one corner, half covered by the billowy waves of hay just swept aside to give them standing-room. Towards evening the cattle are driven in again from grazing, and each herdsman or herdswoman, as the case may be, brings in his or her quota of field-weeds or firewood; and thus with the passing droves, the children playing about, the men and women conveying the *kiltas* or baskets of agricultural produce from the fields, and the household operations of rice-cleaning, oil-pressing, and blanket-weaving, for which occupation there is generally a small covered shed attached to each house, a Kooloo village is one perpetual scene of life and animation. The quaint cottages, with their projecting roofs, stand out sharp and clear against the background of blue sky or green upland, and the plaids of various colours that hang from verandah and roof, contrast well with the wealth of corn or green grass that, according to the season, lies in such abundance all around. Nearly every house, it should be added, has its several beehives, which are let into the walls, the entrance for the bees being by holes cut in the square blocks of wood that form the outer surface of the hives.

The Lahoul village is, for the most part, but a collection of rude huts of mud, stone, and timber, protected by a flat roof, the lower storey being given to the cattle, and, in wet weather, being always filthily dirty: the upper portion of the house, when there are two storeys, is used by the family. In the Chundra valley there are some villages in which the houses are all massed together in a circle; and this plan has doubtless been adopted for the sake of security and warmth in the winter, when this part of the country is ten and twelve feet deep in snow. The most striking, and probably the largest village in Lahoul, is Kardung, situated on a spur of the range to the left of the river Bagha, the houses here being more carefully built than they are elsewhere. Tara Chund, the Negee of Lahoul, resides at Kolung, on the right bank of the Bagha, but his mansion is of a very humble description; and much the same may be said of the cottages of even the wealthier *Zemindars*.

The Spiti house is far from an uncomfortable one, and is both roomy and spacious; few of the villages are of any size, but even in the smallest the poorest classes are lodged in residences that are far from contemptible, and that are very solidly put together. This care in construction is absolutely necessary in a country where the climate is so rigorous for the greater portion of the year. At Losur I put up in a *Zemindar's* house, which may be taken as a sample of the style of dwelling in common use. The one in question occupied an area of some forty square feet, the entrance being by a strong though low wooden doorway, a flight of stone stairs leading to the family rooms up above, very clean and commodious stalls being reserved underneath for the cattle and sheep. The upper storey was composed of a court walled in, the third of which was roofed, and off it lay a spacious apartment, furnished with small windows, protected by wooden shutters, the roof being supported by uprights from the flooring, which, I should add, was scrupulously clean.

When Mr. Egerton was in Spiti he went over a *Zemindar's* house, and writes of it as follows:—"The upper storey consists of three large apartments, all opening on the courtyard or balcony. The outer room is the one usually occupied by the family, and here were the hand-mill, the water-pail, pestle and mortar, teapot, and the other domestic utensils, and the store of parched barley. The room on the left is the dining-room, and is hung round with the best clothes of the family, including sundry cloaks of white sheepskin. The apartment on the right is the chapel or oratory. In this are the images of Lhooang and Losodong, the popular god and goddess, which, unlike the Hindoo goddess Doorgah, are both beneficent deities. In front of the images is a row of some half-dozen little brass basins full of water, ranged on a shelf at their feet; and, a short way off, several lamps, small vessels filled with melted butter, with a bit of cotton wick, and, by the side of the images were some goodly lumps of butter for replenishing them." The walls of a Spiti house (which is often three storeys high), have generally the first three or four feet of stone, and the whole of the remainder of sun-dried bricks a foot and a half long, eight inches wide, and six deep, cemented together with mortar. In no case are the roofs sloping, and this more probably from the difficulty in procuring timber than any dislike to that style of architecture, or necessity for the flat roof, which is universal. Across the walls solid beams of the width of the apartment are placed, and willow or juniper sticks peeled of their bark form the connecting links, tamarisk twigs and earth being placed over the surface and evenly smoothed down: this description of roof in such a dry climate answers all protective purposes. On the top of the roofs are ranged great layers of brushwood for winter consumption, and in some of the houses long poles are inserted in the walls, from which poles flaunt out black yaks' tails. The smoke from the fires colours the ceilings a deep coal-tar hue, for chimneys are no part of the Spiti householder's domestic economy. The upper portions of the walls are daubed on the outside with a grey-coloured marl, and, by way of ornament, broad, irregular bands of red and chrome are traced just under the line of the roof and round the windows. By each house is the open walled-in enclosure for yaks or ponies.

A Spiti village, of the larger class, presents an aspect of bustling activity. Sitting in an upper room, one probably looks out over a steep descent covered with houses, each roof having its serried layers of fagots of dried rose-wood and grass, neatly arranged, something in the form of an *abattis.* The windows of the houses are small, and their shutters are painted in red and deep blue, but with no pretensions to taste. Tier after tier the roofs descend, and both on them, and in the narrow and steep pathways, are generally to be seen a number of men and women and children; the various enclosures being filled with ponies, sheep, yaks or goats. On an adjoining housetop may be noticed women lying down in easy attitudes, while their hair is arranged by friends, in the multitudinous braids affected by the Spiti fair ones. Just below are two *Lama* boys, in ragged red coats, with bare heads, and yellow patches on their dresses, helping an antiquated dame with a load of firewood; while some other lads surround a venerable old Thibetan, probably a wanderer from Lhassa or Shagatze, who twirls his prayer-wheel with one hand, and with the other enforces the point of his argument on his auditors. Further down, sitting under the shade of a huge rock, are several of the gentler sex, their frames stretched before them, working away at the construction of *puttoo* and blankets, or carrying on a laughing conversation with their friends who, may be, here stop to rest, and have, for the moment, disburdened themselves of their baskets, which can be seen leaning against the rock.

It is by no means dull work to one who

keeps his eyes open in a Spiti village; there is plenty that is both interesting and amusing, as I can vouch for, after a pretty tolerable experience in looking from the housetops.

## CHAPTER VI.

**Climate of Kooloo.—Crops in Kooloo.—The Rice, Poppy, and Tobacco Crops.—Tea.—Climate of Lahoul.—Crops in Lahoul.—Climate of Spiti.—Crops in Spiti.—Arboriculture.—Waste Lands.—Domestic Animals.—Wild Animals.—Game Birds.**

IN such a large extent of country as is comprised in this subdivision, the differences of climate and altitude occasion considerable varieties in the seasons for sowing and harvest, and in the descriptions of produce procurable in the various valleys.

Kooloo enjoys a very equable and agreeable climate. In the Upper Beas valley, which may be first discussed, the spring, summer, and autumn are remarkably genial and pleasant; in the winter, the snow that falls heavily as far south as Nuggur, disappears by the beginning or middle of March, and not until the end of June is the temperature by any means oppressive; even then, however, the smallest shelter suffices, and hot winds in this part of the subdivision are quite unknown. In July and August the weather often becomes close and sultry for days together; but in the upper portion of the valley these months are far from disagreeable, and by September, as a general rule, the season is as enjoyable as it can be anywhere out of England. In December the clouds again begin to gather, and before the end of that month all the passes are closed with snow; but this rarely happens until the very end of the year.

In Wuzeeri-Rupi the heat is much greater than in the Upper Beas valley, and the snow falls but seldom low down; in Seoraj there is much the same temperature, but the sun in this part of the district is very powerful, exposure to its rays during the summer months being about as trying as it could be in the early summer in the Punjab.

The rainy season throughout the whole of Kooloo is much less severe than might at first be imagined from its propinquity to the plains; but the lofty ranges that stretch at the back of Kangra break the masses of clouds, and it so happens that in the Upper Beas and Parbuttee valleys, the rain-fall is not at all heavy; the prevailing characteristic of this season being drizzling showers, which pass off, leaving the sky again totally clear, though, of course, there are frequently very heavy falls. In the present year (1870) there has been more continued wet weather, and a greater quantity of rain than any of the present inhabitants of the valley can remember. Thunder and lightning in Kooloo are very uncommon; storms rage along the crests of the mountains, but there they seem to be for the most part localized. In Seoraj, which is not protected by any line of mountains, the monsoons sweep up over the Simla hills, and the fall in consequence is by no means small; but I have not much personal experience of the climate in Seoraj, and therefore I would guard against too authoritative a construction being placed on what I have entered as regards this part of the subdivision. It would be difficult to determine the mean elevation of Kooloo, where even the valleys are so undulating; a few heights of various localities may, however, be recorded here. Menalee, at the head of the Upper Beas valley, is 6,495 feet above sea-level; and Nuggur, in the same tract, is 5,780 feet. Sooltanpore, the chief town, is 4,092 feet in height; Manikurn, in the Parbuttee valley, is 5,587 feet; Bajoura is 3,689 feet; Plach, in Seoraj, is 5,718 feet; and Nirmand, also in Seoraj and close to the Sutledj, is rather over 4,000 feet above sea-level.

Throughout Kooloo, except in the higher vales, the soil yields two crops annually. The main crops are rice, opium, tobacco, wheat, Indian corn, barley, and amaranth; but almost every description of grain grows to perfection, and is thickly cultivated. In May and June rice is sown; in April and May, tobacco; and the poppy in November; the harvest for rice being in September and October; for opium, the end of May; and for tobacco, August and September. A table, given in the Appendix, will place the statistics of these crops better before my readers.

In ploughing, the small oxen of the country are employed, the plough being the common wooden one, pointed with iron.

The potato, the pumpkin, the bean, and a species of lettuce are all grown extensively, and, with European culture, English vegetables approach in excellence the produce of the gardens at home; tomatoes, carrots, lettuce, French beans, peas, artichokes, asparagus, cauliflower, and cabbage being fully equal to the best samples of the English markets. Strawberries of a peculiarly rich flavour have been reared with success in several parts of the Upper Beas valley, and other fruits are numerous. The quince, peach, apricot, plum, grape, pomegranate, apple, fig, pear, nuts, and walnuts, are all common, besides a tasteless species of strawberry; but, with the exception of the walnut, apricot, plum, quince, and in some rare cases the peach and fig, none of these are particularly palatable. Careful gardening, and engrafting, would, however, in a short time produce very different results, for almost every article fit for human food grows to perfection in this country, so bountifully endowed by nature; and it would seem as if Kooloo well deserved the appellation of the Garden of India, so rich is it in all the products that gratify either sight or taste.

Irrigation is much resorted to in Kooloo, and there is but seldom any lack of the needful supply of water for the fields. And the tributaries of the Beas, which throughout the year remain of a considerable size, only join the parent stream after heavy demands have been made upon them; every hill torrent being brought in to aid in the work of irrigation.

The rice crop* is one that is quite dependent on the facility of procuring water, and per-

* For the information here recorded regarding the rice, poppy, and tobacco crops, and the cultivation of tea, I am indebted to Mr. Miniken, the obliging manager of the Kooloo Tea Estate.

haps on the whole necessitates more careful watchfulness and constant labour than any other. In May, a plot of ground varying from thirty to forty feet in circumference is marked off, this is well manured and ploughed, and the surface rendered smooth and even; forty* *pucka* seers of *dhan* (husk rice) are then sown, and the soil is thoroughly drenched with water. In fifteen days the seed germinates, and in June, when about ten inches high, the shoots are ready for transplanting. It is customary to plant wheat, &c., in rice land, and it is when these crops are cleared off in May and June that the soil is prepared for rice, being first ploughed and irrigated, the manure being laid on when the land is partly dry; manuring is not, however, always adopted. Ploughing then again takes place, after which the rough surfaces are levelled with the *mahee*, a thick piece of wood about four feet in length, upon which a man stands or sits and guides the bullocks. The soil

* Forty *pucka* (or full) seers are eighty pounds English.

is then again irrigated and harrowed, and whilst very soft and well flooded, the shoots are taken from the nursery and planted about six inches apart. The men do the ploughing, but the women undertake the planting-out; and in June, in the Upper Beas valley, up to the end of July, these last are to be seen day by day, up to their knees in mud and water, carrying on the work with speed and precision. Each *Zemindar* owning rice-fields obtains the assistance of his friends, and he in turn aids in preparing their fields. It is not unusual to see thirty or forty women working together in two or three adjoining rice-fields, all busy at transplanting the shoots, while the *Zemindar* and his companions sit watching the proceedings; it being customary for the owner of the estate to get together such musicians as he can collect, who play on pipes, and so with melody—in a very minor key, however, and many a laugh and jest, the work progresses. The scene is somewhat of an attractive one. Many of the women are very pretty; and their bright and fanciful head-dresses set off their comely faces; the rich emerald-green of the young rice shoots standing out with great distinctness from the muddy water. No money is ever offered, or would be accepted, for the services rendered, but food is given, usually six *chupatties*, or three seers of *attah*,* daily each female. Towards evening, when the workers are pretty well wet through, and one would think the toil (and very severe toil it is) would result in fatigue, the spirits of the party rise, and the more playful members of the fair sex commence slyly throwing water on those near; this is returned, but usually in the wrong direction, and soon all are busily engaged in pelting each other, till struggles for supremacy occur, and the weakest go bodily into the water; but all is in the purest good-nature, and there are no signs of ill-temper or revengeful feeling, even among those who have come worst off. Sometimes a more than usually audacious damsel

* Six pounds of wheat.

advances to the bank, and before the spectators can be aware of her intentions, one of their number is dragged from his place of safety, and water is poured down his neck, amidst the laughter of the bystanders, who have to be careful that their turn will not come next. Nothing can exceed the ludicrous absurdity of gesticulation on the part of the victim, probably the owner of the field, who entreats his fair captors to do their spiriting gently; but it is not often he is released before he has paid handsomely for not being a little better on the alert. The rice-fields or terraces are irrigated every third or fourth day for about three weeks, and in the mean time, should weeds or grass appear, a harrow with eight or ten teeth is drawn over the field by oxen, and though the rice shoots are turned up with the weeds, the plants are easily readjusted and quickly again take root, whilst the weeds perish. The aspect of the country when the rice has been all planted out is very striking, the enormous extent of vivid green being peculiarly beautiful. The crop is cut in September and October; the straw being stored for fodder in the winter. One *maund*, or eighty pounds of *dhan*, when well cleared of the husk, leaves twenty to twenty-two seers (forty to forty-four pounds) of *chawal* or rice, the selling price of which is Rs. 2 to Rs. 2. 4 a. or Rs. 2. 5 a.* per pucka maund. But little rice is either disposed of to the shopkeepers in Kooloo or consumed by the Kooloo people. The Lahoulees are the great purchasers, and perhaps half of the entire quantity taken over by the latter is made, during their winter stay in Kooloo, into an intoxicating drink called *loogree*. In Kooloo rice is planted from 3,600 to 7,000 feet above sea-level, and from forty-two to forty-six *seers* of seed per acre fourteen to twenty-two *maunds* of dhan are produced. The esteemed kinds of rice are the *basmuttee*, transplanted and irrigated after being sown, *jatoo*, and *sukadass;* these

* Two rupees five annas is about four shillings and sevenpence halfpenny.

last two varieties, of a reddish colour, being the ones more generally sown.

In preparing the ground for poppy cultivation, it is the custom to thickly manure and harrow the soil in November and December, and when it is well pulverized the seed (*post*), about three *seers* to the acre, is then sown broadcast, the shoots appearing in about a fortnight. When nearly a foot high, the weeds and the inferior poppy shoots are cleared away by hand, a space of four inches being left between each remaining plant. Towards the middle of May in Seoraj, and the end of that month in Kooloo proper, the poppy attains perfection; the season of proper ripeness being ascertainable by the change in colour, or by pressing the poppy-head between the finger and thumb, when, should it yield to gentle force, the opium must be extracted. The bulb is then scarified in the afternoon in three places, and early next morning the milk or opium that oozed through the cuts is taken off with a scarifier and placed on a small board; a sufficient quantity of this juice being collected, it is then deposited on poppy-leaves, the only ones that, it is said, are found suitable.

The ensuing evening the bulb is again scarified in other three places, and the opium gathered the following morning, the same process being repeated for the third and sometimes the fourth time. The heads of the plant are then cut off and spread to dry in the sun, the seed (*post*) being taken out. A good crop should give six *maunds* * of seed per acre and yield ten *pucka seers* of oil per *maund* of seed, besides six to eight *seers* of opium. The purchasers of the Kooloo opium are for the most part shopkeepers from Sooltanpore or Mundee, traders from Hooshinpore and Jullundur also dealing largely in the drug, which fetches from Rs. 6 to Rs. 15 per pucka *seer;* the fluctuation in price not so much depending on a short or good crop

* The maund is equal to about eighty pounds English, and contains forty seers of two pounds each.

as on the influx of buyers. The Kooloo *Zemindars* adulterate their opium extensively, though they know their doing this affects the price of the article, for opium that has been tampered with is of a dirty colour, and is easily distinguishable from the better sort; it also loses very much in weight if kept any time. The poppy stalks, or stems, are left in the ground and ploughed in for manure. Red-blossomed poppy produces more opium and less seed than the white, and the seed gives scarcely any oil; but though from the white poppy less opium is extracted, this is of very good quality, and the seed yields much oil. In the upper valley of Kooloo proper the seed is eaten to some extent; but in Seoraj the people partake of it largely. I have no means of ascertaining what quantity of opium is produced in the subdivision—returns say 100 *pucka* maunds, but I should imagine this quotation to be far below the truth.

For tobacco, a field is prepared for the seed in April or May by a system of thorough manuring, ploughing, harrowing, and smoothing the soil; the tobacco seed then being sown by the simple process of blowing it off the hand! When planted in the above months the crop requires irrigation, but this is not had recourse to if the sowing is delayed till the rainy season. Transplanting takes place, according to the nature of the crop, in either June or July, the irrigated crop becoming ripe in August, and the other in September and October. When ripe, the plant is cut down and the leaves twisted round it and left to dry: rain or moisture at this stage is fatal to the worth of the produce. An acre of land well prepared and sown with three and a half *seers* of seed, ought to return from ten to twelve *maunds* of tobacco leaf. The main purchasers of the luxury are Kooloo, Seoraj, and Mundee *Zemindars;* the selling price being from six to eight *seers* per rupee.* This tobacco is liked by some Europeans, but it is not a first-class article, though

* Twelve to sixteen pounds for the two shillings.

this may probably arise from imperfect curing, as the dry leaf has a very mild and pleasant perfume.

The amaranth, called the *surreara,* is a cereal that is grown in great profusion in all unirrigated land, and when the autumn is well on, the deep crimson leaves and heavily-laden stalks present features in the landscape not a little attractable.

Some few remarks may correctly be inserted here on the cultivation of tea in the subdivision. In Kooloo the tea seedlings must not be removed from the nursery until strong and healthy, and they should be at least a foot in height. After transplantation they may be expected to come to perfection in about seven years. At least three times a year the tea-garden should be hoed all over, when all grass and weeds must be carefully removed, and, if possible, irrigation should be had recourse to in April, May, and June. The outlay per acre per annum comes to about fifty shillings, and by the fourth year a plantation may be relied on for a small return, but it cannot be deemed self-supporting till the sixth year.

In the making of tea great care has to be observed, and more than one roasting and rolling of the leaf is necessary if tea of a fine quality is to be turned out. Nor does the labour end here, for the leaf must be well dried over charcoal fires, an operation requiring some skill and nicety in the workmen. When made, the leaf is placed in the storehouses, and should be, as a rule, some months in hand before despatched to customers, it being again heated, and while warm packed in chests for transmission to the plains. The extent of ground laid out in tea in Kooloo is in all about 200 acres; and the produce of the gardens has been always highly esteemed. In the Lahore Exhibition of 1863, the Kooloo Tea Company secured the first prize for the best tea manufactured in the Punjab, with the first prize for the best black tea made in India.

None of the Kooloo tea is disposed of to shopkeepers or dealers; some small quantity is despatched to England, but the majority of the out-turn finds its way to messes in India, or to private constituents, the better sort fetching from Rs. 1. 8 a. to Rs. 2 a pound, a high price, it may be thought; but the article is quite worth the money. The Kooloo Tea Company have plantations at Bajoura, Shumshee, Raesun, Gourdour, and Nuggur.

In Lahoul, spring commences about the middle of April, but snow lies in the upper valleys till late in that month. Towards the close of September frost begins to set in, though the three last months of the year are generally singularly clear and fine. By January dead winter commences, and from then until April the country is covered with snow to a depth of eight and ten feet, the villages in the higher altitudes being completely submerged. The rainfall in Lahoul is usually very small; there are heavy showers now and then in July and August in the lower valleys of the Chundra and Bagha, but wet weather is seldom of long continuance. The climate, on the whole, may be considered singularly dry and bracing; along the upper portion of the Chundra and Bagha rivers the cold, in the summer, is intense; and this is made more unendurable from the bitter winds, which usually spring up before midday, blowing like a hurricane at three or four P.M., and only subsiding into a gentle breeze after the sun has set. The nights are invariably calm and quiet. The main elevation of Lahoul above the sea is computed by Cunningham at 10,535 feet.

In Lahoul grass first appears by the middle of April, and ploughing and sowing take place in May, the harvest being collected in September. The main crops are barley and buckwheat: of the former there are three varieties. Wheat is but rarely reared, and then only in the Chundra Bagha valley: this wheat is said to be of a very fine quality.

A large tap-root, in local phraseology *Ludut*, is occasionally converted into flour, and mixed with barley or buckwheat; but of cultivated vegetables there are none, though the leaves and stem of the dandelion, and such plants, are largely used for culinary purposes; rhubarb also grows wild on all the higher passes. In 1857, the Moravian missionaries at Kielung introduced nearly every kind of European vegetable, which all thrive admirably; but the Lahoulees were too lazy to benefit by the example, and to this day content themselves with such products as they have always had an acquaintance with. Of fruits there are but few. There are wild strawberries, a small cherry, and a sour apple, which, with the wild gooseberry, may be said to represent this class of edibles. Apricots are sparsely grown in the Chundra Bagha valley, but the fruit never ripens at any considerable altitude: there are also a few walnut-trees in the same locality.

The plough in Lahoul is much the same as the one used in Kooloo; this is worked by a pair of *dzōs* (hybrids between the cow and yak). Irrigation is extensively carried out, the waters of every available stream being led by built channels to the fields. Indeed, the supply of rain in the valley is so precarious, that were not recourse had to irrigation, the greater part of the soil would have to lie untilled. Hedges are unknown, but branches of prickly trees are run along the fields, and form good substitutes for fences.

The seasons in Spiti assimilate much to those of Lahoul; but the spring is later, and the winter is, if not more rigorous, of longer duration than in the neighbouring valley. In December the snow begins to fall, and remains on the ground till the end of April; the cold, too, becomes intense, and the streams are all frozen.

In Spiti the rainfall is even smaller than in Lahoul, and showers are very infrequent, this district being almost quite beyond the influence of the monsoons. The climate of Spiti is even more bracing than is that of Lahoul, and, though the days in the short summer are exceptionally hot, yet the nights are almost invariably cold to a degree. The strong winds are very trying to a constitution unaccustomed to their influence, and the visitor who is exposed to their full fury has good cause to remember this, the face and hands, if left exposed, being cut open and abraded, as if with a penknife. The main elevation of the Spiti valley is given by Cunningham at 12,986 feet above the sea.

The soil in Spiti, as in Lahoul, only yields one crop in the year. The main crops are a very fine hexagonal wheat, peas, mustard, and two kinds of barley. Sowing takes place in May, and the harvest in September; in ploughing, the yak, or hybrid between the yak and cow, being always employed. Long channels for the conveyance of water from the hill torrents are to be seen, winding literally for miles along the mountains; and when the supply fails all cultivation dies out. There is much land in Spiti that could be reclaimed from waste were water only procurable.

There are no fruits in Spiti, and, with the exception of peas and mustard, no vegetables. "The diminution of atmospherical pressure," says Captain Hay, in his report on Spiti, "is inimical to the growth of trees," and hence the whole of the country has a singularly bare and barren aspect.

Extensive ranges of forest exist throughout Kooloo, which is also, for the most part, richly wooded. The deodar attains to considerable dimensions in the Upper Beas and Parbuttee valleys, in both of which the Forest Department have establishments for cutting the trees, which are floated down the Beas to the depôts in the plains. All the higher ranges are densely timbered, and, as the valleys attain a greater altitude, the trees descend lower, and mass themselves over the more level ground. Certain of the forests have been given up absolutely to the Forest Department, while others are retained under the control of the civil authorities. The better class of trees in Kooloo are the *deodar*, *kyle*, *cheel*, walnut, horse-chestnut, plane, elm, oak, and box; the mango is unknown, and the *rae*, *tosh*, and alder, though beautiful in an artistic point of view, are almost worthless for building purposes, as they rot when exposed to wet. In Lahoul, the principal trees are the pencil-cedar and the *kyle*, the former of which grows in scattered patches over many of the hill-sides, and the latter in two large forests, the one on the left bank of the Chundra, near Muling village, and the other on the left bank of the Bagha, to the north of Kardung. The hill peepul and willow are common in the lower valleys in Lahoul, and the walnut grows to some size along the banks of the Chundra Bagha; the birch also is numerous in the loftier ranges. The *deodar* has never, I believe, been acclimatized in Lahoul, but the *kyle* affords timber almost equally valuable.

In Spiti there are hardly any trees at all, but towards the southern end of the valley, which I have not visited, there must be specimens of some size procurable, as it cannot be supposed every petty *Zemindar* would carry the beams for his house one by one over the passes which bar the road to every country round in which wood is procurable. Along the upper course of the Spiti willows grow by the left banks of the river, and occasionally a few peepul-trees may be noticed; but these are never cut down, the brushwood, that is tolerably abundant, answering admirably for all purposes of fuel.

The subject of "waste lands" in the subdivision will doubtless have been fully discussed by Mr. Lyall in his Kooloo settlement report, which I have not yet seen, and I hesitate to enter into any details on a matter which hardly lies within my province. But, on more than one occasion, I have been called in to arrange difficulties that have arisen between Europeans who desired to purchase waste, and Zemindars who would not sell. In Kooloo the Government has a lien on all forest and "common" land, though at the same time the villagers retain their own rights, that have been reserved to them within these areas, and they are naturally averse to seeing any limitations put on their power to graze their cattle therein. If plots are sold, the purchase-money has to be divided among such a number of proprietors, that each can only have an infinitesimal proportion, and, as they believe they gain nothing by the transfer of the land, and clearly see they must lose something, as a rule, dissentients are always to be found, who object to the entry of European settlers on "common" lands. I think some steps might be taken to facilitate the acquirement of lots by Europeans who desire to settle in the valley, for it appears to be a monstrous pity to see such thousands of acres, which might easily be utilized, and which are never touched by the people, lying within sight but quite beyond the reach of the would-be settler.

Of domestic cattle in Kooloo there are cattle of a small, poor breed, a few ponies, asses, dogs, sheep, and goats, and in some places poultry are kept; all of the above, with the exception of the last, are to be found in Lahoul, where they have also a tolerably good breed of pony, and the hybrid between the yak and the cow. The same classes of animals are also to be seen in Spiti, though here again both the yak and pony are far superior to those found in Lahoul.

The yak (*Bos grunniens*) that, partially in Lahoul, and almost altogether in Spiti, takes the place of cattle elsewhere, appears to be peculiarly adapted to the climates of the country it inhabits. With an average height of from twelve to thirteen hands, furnished with a very bovine head (much depressed below the line of the back) and fine pair of horns, very long, shaggy coat, and short, strong legs, the yak presents an appearance of immense power, to which the wild glare of the eye adds an aspect of rude ferocity, and it is probable that, in his native plains, the latent viciousness of his disposition must make him, when caught at mature age, perfectly unmanageable. In colour these animals are nearly always black, but their tails, of a fine silky wool, are frequently grey, or of a creamy white, and these tails, termed *chowries*, which fetch from 2*s*. to 6*s*. apiece, form an article of export, and are used not only by all hill rajahs on occasions of ceremony, but also in viceregal durbars, where it is the custom to wave a pair of chowries, richly set in silver handles, over the enthroned representative of the British empire in the East. In Lahoul and Spiti it is usual to cross the yak with the cow, and the hybrid is deemed a better animal both for the plough and dairy, the milk of the hybrid cow being more plentiful and far richer and sweeter than that procurable from either the female yak or pure cow. Accustomed to a climate where bitter cold is the normal state of the country it usually inhabits, to the yak the severe winter of Spiti and Lahoul causes no inconvenience, and, with snow deep on the ground, this animal is allowed to wander at will and find its own pasture, which it very cleverly secures by scraping up the snow. A few specimens of the yak have been brought down into the Punjab, and one was shown in the Lahore Exhibition in 1863, as also at the first Palumpore Fair in 1867; but it will not live long below an elevation of 10,000 feet; at this altitude it degenerates, it is said, and all attempts at domesticating it, even in the highest parts of Kooloo, have quite failed, enlargement of the liver resulting, after a limited stay, in even a tolerably cool climate.

In Kooloo the brown and black bear, the spotted and white leopard, ibex, musk deer, wild cat, flying squirrel, hyæna, wild pig, jackal, fox, and marten are all to be found; in Lahoul the same varieties of bear, the ibex, wolf, and marmot; and in Spiti the wild goat, the nabboo or burral, and occasionally a stray leopard or wolf.

In game birds Kooloo is particularly favoured; every description of hill pheasant abounds, but the *minal* and the *argus*, as elsewhere, are only procurable in the highest ranges. The white-crested pheasant (*kalidj*) the *koklās*, and the *cheer*, with red junglefowl, black and wood partridge, and *chikor* are common in the lower hills; snipe, wood-cock, and teal, with quail in the lower grass ground, being also tolerably abundant. In winter the *golind* or snow pheasant, and the snow partridge, can be obtained without difficulty, and at this season of the year wild duck and wild geese may also be secured. Eagles, vultures, kites, and hawks inhabit the upper fastnesses, and occasional specimens of these have been secured by bird-fanciers. In Lahoul game birds are rarer than in Kooloo, but the *minal*, *golind*, and *chikor* of two varieties have been shot in that valley. With the exception of the *golind*, no game birds are procurable in Spiti, where, however, the blue rock pigeon, as in Kooloo and Lahoul, is common.

## CHAPTER VII.

**Religious Edifices in the Subdivision. — Religion in Kooloo.—Varieties of Temples in Kooloo.—Tree and Serpent Worship.—Buddhism and Hinduism. —Religion in Lahoul.—Religion in Spiti.—Lamas and Nuns.—Buddhistical Implements, &c.**

ONE very striking peculiarity in this subdivision is the great number of religious edifices which, either as Hindoo temples or Buddhist monasteries, are scattered broadcast over the country. In Kooloo there is scarcely a village that has not its sacred shrine or idol-house; and in several cases there are many of these collected together, each of which has its select body of worshippers, and their separate lands held on rent-free tenures from the State.

Throughout Kooloo (inclusive of the Upper Beas valley, Wuzeeri-Rupi, and Seoraj) the faith is Hinduism; but it is not the religion of the orthodox, who, however, visit all the celebrated Kooloo shrines, though they have but small regard for the creed of their hill brethren, whose tenets they hold in derision. Besides Hinduism, serpent-worship, as will be presently shown, is also practised. Mr. Lyall, late Settlement-Officer of Kangra, gave some interesting information about the Kooloo gods, in a paper which has been published, and which forms No. XXXIII. of "Selections from the Records of the Punjab Financial Commissioners' Office." He divides the Kooloo gods into Deos, Davees, Rikhis, Munis, Jognees, and Nâgs, the latter being the snake gods, Jognees forest fairies, and Rikhis and Munis men who have attained to divine honours by their ascetism or great deeds. "Of the Deos or Davees," he says, "a few bear names well known in Hindoo mythology;" but, for the most part, they take the appellation given them in the village where their temples lie. The religion of the majority of the Kooloo people is a sort of demon-worship, which may be deemed an offshoot of the Hindoo creed. All hold in honour the greater names of the Hindoo mythology, and reverence the temples that contain statues of the noticeable gods; but their affections are more particularly concentrated on their own local deities, whose help they invoke in trouble, and by whom they swear when taking an oath. The *Poojarees* are the worshippers or priests at the temples, and these men are found attached to all shrines in the higher ranges. On great festivals, when fairs are held, and all the people are gathered together, it is the part of these priests to flog themselves (but very gently) with steel chains, to go through certain pantomimic actions with a sword, with food, and fire, and then to take up a position under some wide-spreading tree, where, like a modern Delphic oracle, they, being then fully inspired, answer any questions the ignorant crowd may put to them. All the temples have priests, and the better class have a regular relief of Brahmins, who take it in turn to attend to the cleanliness of the building and the performance of the proper daily services. The Brahmins as a class are, in Kooloo, childishly superstitious; but the common people, though, on the whole, satisfied with their faith, are not slavishly bound by it; and, as an instance, it may be mentioned they never hesitate to kill snakes, although the serpent is supposed to be an object of adoration all over the country. A religion which inculcates attendance at Melas, and such-like orgies, is a creed that does not fail to recommend itself to the simple peasant, for it costs him nothing to keep up the worship in the temples, which all have their rent-free grants; and where the tenets of Hinduism cross his fancy, he treats these as if they had no existence.

There are throughout Kooloo three, if not four, distinct species of temple, which probably may mark different eras of religious belief; and, perhaps, the infusion of new races with the older inhabitants. In the great dearth, however, of written records of the history of the country, and with the very slight notice taken by Indian writers of this out-of-the-way part of the world, there are but few clues that can be relied on as guides to any changes in the phases of past creeds. The varieties of temples are as follows :—

1st. The pyramidal carved stone temple, which is also common in India.

2nd. The rectangular stone and wood temple, furnished with a pent roof and verandah.

3rd. The rectangular stone and wood temple, provided, pagoda fashion, with successive wooden roofs, one on the top of the other.

4th. The small rectangular temple, with a pent roof; this being probably but a variety of the edifices of the second order above quoted.

It would be difficult to determine which of these is the most ancient. Of the first there are not many, considering the extent of country in which they are to be found; in all, I believe, there are but sixteen, which are situated as below :—

1 near Munglor, in Seoraj.

1 at Bajoura, Lower Beas valley.
1 ,, Mukraha, in ditto.
1 ,, Manikurn, in Wuzeeri-Rupi.
1 ,, Sooltanpore, the chief town in Kooloo.
4 ,, Nuggur, in Upper Beas valley.
1 ,, Chakee, in ditto.
2 ,, Sursai, in ditto.
2 ,, Juggutsookh, in ditto.
1 ,, Shooroo, in ditto.
1 ,, Basisht, in ditto.

Of these the Bajoura one is at once the most notable for its ornate carvings, and the figures portrayed on the outer walls and entrance are, I think, certainly equal to anything of the sort I have seen elsewhere in India.*

The other specimens are all inferior to this one, not in size, for some are larger, but in the execution of details. As to the time of erection of this class of building there is but little to guide one to a correct decision; but

* For a fuller account of the Bajoura temple, see Chap. XIV.

it is not improbable that they only date back to the reign of Rajah Juggut Sing, who is said to have reigned in Kooloo about 1640–70, and who is known to have had the idol of Rugonath brought from Oudh to Kooloo. The popular belief is, that this chief built all the stone temples in the country, and it is positively asserted that he erected the one at Basisht; nor is it unlikely that the majority of these edifices, always excepting the one at Bajoura, were constructed either in his reign or in the times of his successors. Again, it is not improbable that he merely revived the worship of Vishnoo, which, it has been said, was not known before his era; and it may well be that some few of these temples are of a much more ancient date than the people of Kooloo credit. One argument in favour of this view, is the existence of one of them at Mukraha, once a populous village, and perhaps one of the oldest in Kooloo, but which has been deserted, I believe, for centuries. Several of these temples are covered at the top with a curiously square timbered roof, that spreads over the main building like a fan.

The rectangular stone and wood temples, with pent roofs, I am inclined to regard as a class as the most ancient in Kooloo. These are scattered all over the country, and though, in every instance brought to my notice, their upper portions have been repaired, it would seem as if the groundwork of all must have been laid at a very remote period. In size these structures vary considerably; but while they differ in the construction of their verandahs, and the amount of carved work with which they are laden, they all have one common feature, and this is, the finely-cut, large, and excellent stones that constitute their base. Perhaps the most remarkable of these temples is the one at Bijli Mahadeo, 8,076 feet above sea-level, which is situated on the extreme western spur of the range that flanks the right bank of the Parbuttee river. This temple is both large and very substantially built, being thirty-six feet in length by twenty-four in breadth. The lower portion of the walls is of cut stone, no plaster being used throughout. A covered verandah of carved *deodar* encircles the building, and the sloping roof is formed of six tiers of planks of the same wood, being protected at the top by a long beam, on which are placed small blocks that are ornamented with tridents. At the entrance, which is to the west, there are fancifully carved uprights, that join on to the roof, and a good deal of open carving also surrounds the arched windows in the fretted verandah. Before the doorway are some heaps of stone-work, and two rudely sculptured stone bulls, while to the north of these rises a lofty beam of *kyle* (*Pinus excelsa*) that is sunk into the ground and secured by huge wedges. The height of this pole is about sixty feet; and from the statements of the priests it is to be gathered that it has to be renewed every two years, as within this period it is always struck by lightning, which, curiously enough, is very prevalent in this locality, though almost unknown throughout the Upper Beas valley. Adjacent to the main building is a *dhurmsala*,* that is used by those who come to pay their respects to the presiding deity, who is Mahadeo; but the lofty pole to the right front of the entrance is nothing more than a *lât*, such as is to this day erected before Buddhist temples in Ceylon; and at one time this structure may have been also a Buddhist place of worship. I have been unable to discover when this edifice was constructed.

There are many other temples very similar in form to the one just noticed, but to attempt any detailed description of these would occupy too much space. I may, however, allude to the Juggutsookh temple, which has some good carvings and statues in the interior; and it is on the outer portal of this building that a sentence is recorded which would apparently point to the name of the sovereign in whose reign it was built. The inscription, although engraved on very hard stone, is almost illegible, and it was only

* A resting-place for travellers.

after pencilling over the outline and taking a careful copy on paper from the original, that I was enabled to place the character before those who could decipher the writing, which, as far as I can gather, has never yet been read off. The sentence runs as follows:—"Sirree Maharajah Oodun Pal sundya Davee kalee Moorut hai." Now, Oodhun Pal was the eighty-third in descent from and the seventy-fifth successor to the throne of Behungamunnee, and seems to have ruled in Kooloo only two before Sidh Sing, whose date of accession is quoted at A.D. 1321;* so in all probability this temple was erected somewhere to the close of the thirteenth century. There are some further inscriptions in this temple which I have not been able to get translated. They will be found in the Appendix, as copied by me from the walls. Outside are the remains of several small pyramidal stone temples arranged in rude order; but these may have been placed in position by

* No reliance can be placed on the correctness of this date.

worshippers who preferred to honour the oldest shrine, and who brought to it as ornaments the fragments of buildings erected by those who had the power to command the adoption of a new creed. On the other hand, however, it would not be difficult to assert that at the construction of the Juggutsookh temple, of order No. 2, these relics of a more ancient shrine were brought forth and arranged as they now lie. For a more detailed description of the carvings at Juggutsookh I must refer my readers to Chapter XIV.

Of the rectangular temples with the pagoda-like roof, surmounted by a cupola, there are, I believe, but four in Kooloo, and apparently all can lay claim to considerable age. The one at Dhyar, on the left bank of the Beas, between Sooltanpore and Bajoura, is believed to be the very oldest temple in Kooloo; but the grounds for this belief I have never been able to ascertain. It is dedicated to Treejogenerain. The others are at Nuggur and Doongree, in the Upper Beas valley, and at Teenun village, in Wuzeeri-

Rupi. The first of these is alluded to in the records of the reign of Busuda Pal, the eleventh chief or Pal of Kooloo, but the reference was as likely as not made very long after this ruler's decease, and was only mentioned at all to show that Busuda Pal once resided near to the place where the edifice now stands. The Doongree temple is perhaps the most notable in all Kooloo, but it is said to be only about 200 years old. A full description of this structure is given in Chapter XIII.

Smaller shrines are found everywhere, either buried in some wooded recess of the mountains, and close to a cascade, or nestling under the village cedars. The local deities are held in high esteem; but the temples consecrated to their use are often mere barns, perhaps a few pointed stones being the only marks to denote the presence of the Divinity. This class of building, built almost entirely of timber, seems to be of a more modern period than any of the others.

Attached to many of the temples are

treasure-houses, in which are kept the musical instruments the *rath*, a species of sedan-chair for the god, and the gold and silver masks that are put over the idol on ceremonious occasions.

The hot springs at Manikurn, in the Parbuttee valley, and at Basisht, two miles north of Menalee, on the left bank of the Beas, are provided with temples; but the hot spring at Khelat, half-way between Sooltanpore and Menalee, on the right bank of the same river, is not so honoured. (See also Chap. XIII.)

The difference between Hinduism and Buddhism is explicitly stated by Marshman, in page 11, vol. i., of his "History of India." He says, "The Buddhists rejected the whole of the Brahminical system of gods and goddesses, repudiated the doctrine of caste, and adhered closely to the spiritual worship of the Vedas.* The priesthood among them

* This is not, strictly speaking, correct, as the snake- and tree-worship that Buddhism engrafted on itself is by no means warranted by the Vedic writings.

was not hereditary, but formed a distinct community, recruited from the regular ranks, bound to observe a vow of celibacy, and to renounce the pleasures of sense. The hereditary priesthood of the Brahmins, on the contrary, admitted no accessions from the lay classes, and considered marriage as indispensable as investiture with the thread, in the hope of giving birth to a son who should perform the funeral rites of his father, and secure him a seat in Paradise."

There is everything to prove that Buddhism, and in all probability a Buddhism that grew out of and was incorporated with tree- and serpent-worship once flourished in Kooloo. The same Buddhistical symbols as have been found in the Sanchi and Amravati scriptures are not by any means uncommon in the district under notice, though, as might be expected, the carvings in the latter do not equal those of the more southern temples. The Buddhistical wheels on the ceiling of the Juggutsookh pent-roofed temple, at Doongree temple, at Huttee village, and close to Shumshee village, besides other places, show, with the rude lion-like but now broken figures, and the effigies of Buddhistical animals, birds, and snakes still to be found here and there, that at no very distant period the creed of Buddha had at any rate its votaries in Kooloo. And if a still further corroboration of this idea be required, it is to be found in the curious sacrifice which at every twelfth yearly feast at Nirmand there takes place, when the victim is swung down a rope that is secured at one end to a lofty rock, and on the other to the ground, the procedure here being identical with that detailed by one of Major Montgomerie's pundits, who witnessed just such a religious exhibition at Potolah fort outside Lhassa, the head-quarters of the Buddhist creed. (For a detailed account of this sacrifice, see Chap. XIII.) Buddhism, according to Fergusson, joined tree- and subsequently serpent-worship with itself; and it is a fact not to be ignored that to this day, in one form or another, serpent-worship is a feature of the religious belief of the people of this subdivision. What the very oldest creed was in India it would be next to impossible to determine; we know that subsequent to the Vedic age, which had nought to do with the monstrosities of the modern Hindoo Pantheon, the whole land was, according to the best authorities, immersed in a blind worship of snakes and trees, and that Buddhism reared up its stately fabric from out of the discordant elements that lay at hand. From the year 623 B.C. it steadily increased in importance till the ninth or tenth century of the Christian era, when it was driven almost completely out of India, and doubtless took refuge in the Himalayan valleys, its last standing-point, till finally expelled altogether from the limits of Hindostan. Then followed Hinduism, and with it uprose the hydra-headed multitude which constitute the gods of the Hindoo of our age. The older the temple, the more strikingly are to be seen in juxtaposition the emblems of each succeeding faith; but one archæological clue we have which is not a little valuable, and that is, as pointed out by the learned Fergusson, that prior to the Buddhistical period not a stone temple was ever built in Hindostan. All the more ancient edifices bear the marks of the Buddhists side by side with the disfigured remains of snakes, which have been set aside for the more modern deities which crowd the religious imagination of a people, of whom it may with truth be said they know not whom they worship. Whether snake-adoration was the primal creed of Kooloo, I do not undertake to say; there are as many arguments for this view of the case as for the assertion that serpent-worship only came in with Buddhism; but to this day there are many temples in Kooloo dedicated to the *Nag*, to whom are attributed divine powers; the effigies of serpents being profusely cut either in wood along the lintels of the doorways, or iron casts of the same being screwed into the woodwork of the door-posts. Nor can these carvings be for a moment understood to be mere ornamentations put on without meaning. True it is, that in Kooloo the *Zèmindars* will as often as not kill a snake, for I have seen them do this more than once; but they, at the same time, regard it as a god as long as it is either in the tank, or under the stones of the temple, or its effigy is attached to the walls of any religious edifice. In the Solung valley, and in many parts of the Upper Beas valley, in the Surburri valley, and in Wuzeeri-Rupi and Seoraj, there are temples dedicated to snakes, associated, it is true, in some cases with other divinities, but occasionally simply and solely to the honour of the serpent; and this is a fact that, I believe, has not been till now generally known. Fergusson, in his valuable work on Tree- and Serpent-Worship, never alludes to the possibility of the snake being reverenced as a god within the Kangra hills; but hereabouts, I believe, more evidence could be found of this ancient superstition than in any other part of India. In Mundee hill state and in Bara Bunghal, an offshoot of the Kangra Deputy-Commissionership, in

Chumba, and notably in Cashmere, serpent-worship is still in force, and doubtless exists much nearer down to the plains than most of us would credit.

Tree-worship is also followed in Kooloo, though that is not extraordinary, as in many parts of India certain trees are considered sacred and have oblations offered before them. At Juggutsookh, in the Upper Beas valley, there is a tree near the bungalow, belonging to General Coninghame, which is covered with crooked nails, driven in by those who suffer any pain, and the shepherds of the country are known to tender weekly sacrifices before such trees as are supposed to be able to afford protection to their flocks. In Lahoul, the pencil-cedar is a special mark of adoration; and there are certain bushes which are regarded as sacred, and which the people object to seeing injured. Moorcroft alludes to this matter in his Travels through Lahoul; and the feeling as regards the divine nature of the pencil-cedar is far from having died out. But it may be said there is less veneration for trees in Lahoul than there used to be; and a large *peepul* that grew near the Mission-house in Kielung, and was considered a sort of guardian angel to children, a number of whom annually held a festive gathering underneath it, was, by the desire of the Lahouls themselves, cut down about two years ago.

I am inclined to think that, except in certain special localities, tree- and serpent-worship is gradually dying out in Kooloo and Lahoul, and of its existence in Spiti I am not aware. There remains still the reverence that clings to an old belief, but few have any actual faith in the divine power of either the tree or the serpent. It is a subject of great regret to me that I did not make this very curious phase of religion a greater object of inquiry; but I knew little of its importance till it was too late to acquire much information on this interesting topic.

In Lahoul the religion is essentially Buddhism, with an admixture of Hinduism, but the former has not always existed; for before it became the popular creed, there was a species of belief that went under the title of *Loong pai chos* (or the religion of the valley), which appears to have consisted mainly of bloody human sacrifices to evil spirits; nor has Buddhism, a faith which tolerates no blood-shedding, ever been able to entirely drive out this system of worship. It is true that no human sacrifices at this time take place, but goats and sheep are offered up before trees when watercourses are opened in the spring, or in festivals at the beginning of harvest: all this is quite contrary to the spirit of Buddhism.* It may be said that in Lahoul there are three religions—first, Buddhism; second, Hinduism; third, Loong pai chos. And connected with these there is also caste, which is not in accord with the tenets of Buddha. The distinctions of caste are formally adhered to wherever Hinduism prevails, and where Buddhism reigns its votaries

* The Rev. Mr. Heyde, of Lahoul, was good enough to furnish me with a paper on the religions of Lahoul, of which this is a résumé.

profess to keep caste, but, in reality, do not do so, cow's flesh, for instance, being eaten in secret by Lahoulees. Even where Hinduism is not rampant, respect is paid to Buddhist prejudices, and yaks can be and are allowed to be killed in sacrifice without remonstrance. Every three years in Yanampell or Yampee a yak is slaughtered, and each *kothee* in Lahoul takes it in turn to supply the animal for the sacrifice; and this fact shows pretty clearly that the three religions are blended together to a certain extent; for, along the Chundra Bagha, the prevalent creed is Hinduism, against the faith of which it would be to kill the yak (*Bos grunniens*), as it is in like manner against the dogmas of Buddha; not because Buddhists hold the cow in veneration, but because all taking away of life is prohibited to them.

Again, each creed has its own peculiar superstitions, that are respected by the other two, and in Hinduized Lahoul there are spots marked off as the abode of demons, and all agree in regarding such places with awe and veneration. Hinduism and Buddhism are known to have certain points in common, and Buddha is said by Hindoos to have been the ninth incarnation of Vishnoo. But, though assimilating in some respects, the two faiths, as before detailed, are yet very unlike, and the adherents of either are more widely apart from each other than are Roman Catholics or Protestants, and not only are their religious ceremonials dissimilar, but they commence their new year on separate dates.

From Koksur down the Chundra and up the Bagha to the last village, Darcha, Buddhism prevails, but, from the junction of these two rivers down the Chundra Bagha valley, Hinduism is the creed of the inhabitants, though this again is mixed up with Buddhism. It is not uncommon, in cases of severe sickness, to call in a *Lama* and a *Brahmin*, who both perform their rites, and their mutual advocacy is not unfrequently solicited in the event of misfortunes or severe losses.

In Lahoul there are, in all, perhaps eight small monasteries, and in these books and idols are kept, *Lamas* being the priests and Buddha the chief god. Among the Hindoos Mahadeo is the favourite divinity, there being several temples in his honour, in which *Brahmins* officiate.

The Loong pai chos creed, although it has no place of worship unless the trees or rocks held in reverence can be deemed to be such, has numerous followers, and in many of its rites neither *Brahmins* nor *Lamas* would assist; as, for instance, in the case of slaughter of animals before the pencil-cedar, or at the opening of a watercourse. And not only is it among the lowest classes that this mysterious demon-worship prevails, for even the *Thakoors* of Lahoul are impregnated with the superstitions of the commoner people, and to this day worship idols which have no connection with either Buddhism or Hinduism. One rite of the *Loong pai chos* takes place annually. It is a matter of custom that no grass in Lahoul should be cut with anything but a wooden or horn sickle till a certain fit day has been pronounced; a goat is then killed, and, after that, an iron instrument may be used; and so superstitious are the leading men, who are not otherwise unintelligent, that any servant in their establishments found guilty of disobedience in this matter is most severely punished.

In countries where Buddhism is rampant, the eldest son succeeds to the paternal property, and all the younger sons become Lamas or priests, but in Lahoul, as may be imagined, where there are three conflicting creeds so closely bound up together, this arrangement is not fully carried out. Mr. Lyall, in his census report of Lahoul, mentions that there are only seven real *Lamas* in Lahoul who have no other occupation; but he adds that 1,100 of the *Zemindars* are also *Lamas*, who marry and cultivate land, and have very little of the monk about them. There were, in 1868, no less than seventy-one nuns in Lahoul who could both read and write, and one of these can calculate an eclipse. All the *Lamas* can read and write. "Every woman or girl among the Buddhists can become a nun. Generally," says the Rev. Mr. Heyde, from whom I quote, "the parents decide whether their daughter is to be one or not when she is still quite a young child. In Lahoul no particular ceremonies or rites are observed when a girl enters the religious order; her hair is cut quite short, and she wears thenceforth a red cap, and is bound to learn to read a little. Here the nuns have not, as in Thibet, proper cloisters of their own; they are attached to the monasteries, in which they live only during winter for one or two months. They may also quit their order either to marry (they frequently do marry *Lamas*) or for other reasons." The above clearly shows what a debased Buddhism it must be in Lahoul; for *Lamas* are, by nature of their office, vowed to celibacy, except in the case of particular sects. In Lahoul, however, nearly all *Lamas* are married.

In Spiti, the religious faith is a purer Buddhism than it is in Lahoul; but here also *Loong pai chos* prevails, though to a much smaller extent than in the neighbouring valley. Mr. Lyall reported, in 1868, that there were then 382 Lamas in Spiti, who were attached to five large monasteries, at one of which, the Peen, the monks belong to an order that permits marriage, the residents in the four others being all celibates. The monasteries in Spiti * are very large, and have offshoots at the villages, in which, for the summer time, the majority of the clerics reside with their fathers or brothers, aiding in farm-work or in the carriage of travellers' goods. Mr. Lyall also mentions that there are nineteen families of strolling monks, called *Borans*, who act plays and chant legends. There are only some eight or ten nuns in Spiti, and several of these live at home with their parents. All younger sons in this valley are *Lamas*, and, except

* For an account of a Spiti monastery, see Chap. XIII.

they belong to sects not celibate, cannot marry; whereas, in Lahoul, all younger sons do not necessarily become clerics, and, as before stated, even those that are *Lamas* do not hesitate to enter into matrimonial connections. In Spiti there are, at times, scenes of gross debauchery in the monasteries, a state of things which can be believed when *Lamas* and nuns are living promiscuously together. As the *Lamas* grow older, they are reported to begin to think more of religion, but instances of this sort are not by any means common.

Buddhism has existed longer in Spiti than in Lahoul; and whereas, in the latter valley, there is no recognized local head of the religion, in Spiti there is a primate, called the head *Gelong*, under whom are five other Gelongs, all the other priests being *Lamas* or *Chelas* (neophytes). The two last can be made in Spiti, but for the attainment of the higher rank of *Gelong*, which may be said to be pretty well synonymous with abbot, the candidate has to visit either Tashihumpo or Lhassa for the necessary degree.

Nearly every pious Buddhist has his prayer-wheel, which he twirls round as he engages in conversation, and in all the monasteries are large vat-like cylinders, that revolve on an iron axis, one complete revolution answering for the utterance of all the devotional exercises within. Nor can the long lines of low wall called *Manees*, fail to attract attention: these often extend for many hundred yards, and are covered with loose stones, on which are inscribed the mystical *om mani padmi hom*, or long *slokes* in the Thibetan character. They are deposited as votive offerings by those who desire to have some particular desire granted, or as thank-offerings for answers to bygone expectations. In addition to the above, the *Chhodtens* and *Dungtens* are also worthy of note, and are frequently found just outside monasteries or the larger villages. The *Chhodten* dedicated to the holy Buddha is very similar in form to the *Dungten*, which is a relic-receptacle built in honour of Buddhist saints, whose bones are supposed to be inside. These structures in Spiti and Lahoul generally consist of a square block of whitewashed masonry on a pediment, on the top of which block rise steps in tiers, crested by a rounded mass of stonework, from which ascends a piece of timber, carved in circles, and which is ornamented at the top by some artistic design.

## CHAPTER VIII.

**Amusements of the People.—Melas or Fairs.—Character of the People in Kooloo, Lahoul, and Spiti.—Polygamy and Polyandry.**

THE amusements of the people in the subdivision are not numerous. In many villages in Kooloo the men and boys may be seen playing what might be called hockey, but which, in reality, is simply a game of knocking about a worsted ball with sticks in a promiscuous manner. There is also a species of bear-baiting, that is in vogue among the children. One boy is seated on the ground, and holds a long waistcloth, which is grasped at the other extremity by the lad acting as bear-leader, whose business it is to rush after and beat off the other players, who may attempt to bonnet the bear.

In Spiti the people are fond of horse-racing, dancing, and gambling, and there are often large feasts in the monasteries, where the majority of the revellers get hopelessly drunk, as they do in similar bouts in Lahoul. Music and dancing are much appreciated in Spiti; and the strolling monks are said to act a species of play, but I have never witnessed any of their performances. The sexes do not dance together; the males sometimes join hands; but the women, according to Egerton, place one arm "round the right-hand neighbour's waist, and the other on the left-hand neighbour's shoulder." The pace in these dances is first slow, but rapidly increases in speed, and ends in violent stamping. At page 31 of Egerton's "Tour in Spiti," there is the following amusing account of some horse-races he was invited to witness. "The race-course was the dry bed of a small lake, about 800 yards in circumference. We were preceded there by a cavalry band, making the most discordant noise." The Spiti men then made themselves comfortable under a wall that kept off the wind, and commenced drinking *chang*,* while the Nono and his guests were "served from a private vessel resembling a huge brass teapot." At last, the Nono's eldest son and some of the richer villagers commenced "a dance, to the sound of a flageolet and kettledrums. This dancing was the most ludicrous thing I ever saw, not excepting the races that succeeded. It was a kind of solemn pacing, or rather sidling, to the time of the music, making great play with a long scarf, which was kept extended with both hands, and one end swung over either arm alternately. But the steps! Never talk of the light fantastic toe again. One foot being raised and poised for a moment, is put down as if on eggs, side foremost, with the *heel* well down; and the other foot whipped up, as if something had burnt it, poised, and put down in the same way, the scarf working all the time; and in this manner they move

* *Chang* is the popular spirit in Spiti, and is somewhat similar to the *loogree* of Kooloo.

along, first in single file, and afterwards holding hands in a circle. I think it was the huge, ungainly boots, contrasted with the mincing manner, that made the thing so laughable. After this the racing began, every body starting where he liked, pushing his wretched pony to a gallop, and coming in anywhere. The rider leans quite over the pony's head (so that if declared to win by a nose, it must be the rider's and not the pony's nose), and keeps himself in that position by holding the bridle with both hands, close to the bit. As the *Nono's* son was riding a course, the bridle broke, and down he came on the ground; and the same thing occurred to another."

There are plenty of opportunities for the males in Kooloo to engage in out-door sports, as for a considerable portion of the year agricultural operations are suspended, or are conducted almost entirely by the weaker sex, who do all the rice-planting, and the majority of the household work. But the Kooloo *Zemindar* (and this applies, in the main, to the men in the Upper Beas valley) prefers to sit idle and smoke, or frequent the *loogree* shop.

The *melas* or fairs may, however, be properly classed among the national amusements. At such gatherings, with the exception of those at Sooltanpore, Plach, and Nirmand (for a description of which see Chap. XIII.), nothing is sold, these gala days, which are numerous, being merely of a festive character. Almost every village of any size has its *mela;* and in the more important of these, nominally held in honour of the local *deota, davee,* &c., the people collect in considerable numbers. The scene is a highly attractive one. The village divinity is brought from either the temple or treasure-house, and decked with his silver or gold mask, and dressed out with petticoats and flowers; placed on the *rath* or sedan-chair, it is then carried on the shoulders of two men, preceded by attendants, beating drums and blowing through enormously long and curved trumpets of brass or copper. Behind follow the males in procession, every one being ornamented with garlands. The *rath* being now placed on one side, a space is cleared in the vicinity of the temple for the dancers, who move in a circle round the musicians seated in the centre; and, as the noise of the tomtoms and pipes increases, the performers, worked up into a proper enthusiasm, and all following the motions of a fugleman, commence a species of nautch-like movement, the wands, with which all are provided, being waved simultaneously as the leader may direct. The gestures are not ungraceful,—they are the contrary, grace carried to absurdity; and every dancer endeavours to excel in *pose* and the elegance of his attitudes. On these occasions all are dressed in their best, the men and boys in their newest coats and caps, and any little accessories in the way of coloured scarfs they can adjust about their persons; and the women don every scrap of jewellery and ornament they are able to collect; both sexes being literally covered with garlands of flowers. The effect is certainly pleasing, but the astounding and discordant tumult of the drums and most ear-piercing pipes is anything but an enjoyment to the cultivated ear. While the men are dancing, the women and the male lookers-on are seated round, squatting on every housetop from whence a good point of view can be obtained; and a more striking picture can hardly be conceived than is represented at this time, with the *Deota* and dancers half-buried in flowers, and the women in their brilliant attire, in which there is almost every combination of colour. Meanwhile the priests of the shrine perform their part in the duties of the day; and after going through some meaningless ceremonies, which include playing with a sword and gentle chastisement of their persons with steel chains, they are then in a properly inspired state, and are ready to give replies to any who may desire to essay their prophetic talents. The buffoonery of the *Brahmins* is fully matched by the credulity and simplicity of the people; and it may be conceived what an instrument for harm this pretended power is in the hands of an unscrupulous priest, who may refuse to grant any particular prayer, unless some wish of his own is not previously complied with.* As night approaches the feasting commences, and the women take up the dancing, the revelry now becoming fast and furious. *Loogree*, the pernicious drink made from fermented rice, is imbibed in large quantities; and what, in the afternoon, was a gay and brilliant gathering, soon degenerates into a gross debauch.

These *melas* or fairs are, although to a certain extent religious, entertainments in

* The reflection has occurred to me when witnessing these festivals, how can the people afford to waste so much time? for *melas* are, in some seasons, of daily occurrence; and, secondly, how very well off they must be! for there is not a woman to be seen who has not got her Rs. 70 or Rs. 80 worth of jewellery on, to say nothing of the excellent clothing of the men. Surely the assessment cannot sit very heavily on a people who can thus waste a good half of the year in revelry, and who are better dressed than any peasantry probably in the world.

which all the people can join, and were they without their never-failing accompaniments of drunkenness and immorality, they might be said to serve a not unuseful purpose; but the intoxication, and its consequences, lead to quarrelling, strife, and the breaking up of the closest family ties; and so bad an effect has this horrible liquor *loogree* on the constitution, that the evil results are with difficulty shaken out of the system; and while they remain, the victim is quite incapacitated from anything like toil or hard labour.

It is undoubtedly the case that the frequency of these *melas* is most hurtful to the well-being and moral tone of the people; at present they can hardly be said to answer any end at all, and the crowd, with nothing to do but to sit and look at the dancers,* amuses itself by drinking. When to this are added the excitements of the occasion, the

* In Seoraj and Wuzeeri-Rupi no spirituous liquors are ever drunk; the vicious conduct here commented on is more particularly confined to Kooloo proper.

close contact of the sexes, the glaring of the torches, the demoniacal noise of the music, and the incitements of the unbounded profligacy so common in the Upper Beas valley, it can be understood at once that it would be highly satisfactory could some checks be put to the frequency of such gatherings.

It is certainly to be desired that some impetus should be given towards a desire for proper amusements, and the boys in the schools have been to some extent instructed in various games; nor do I think it altogether a waste of time to devote an hour or two daily to a child's pleasure. Games are of practical utility, and can be made to serve a nobler end than that of mere pastime for idle hours; for, if properly conducted, they are valuable aids to the creation of a good morality; and a lesson (even in the play-ground) inculcated in early life, teaches a lad that honest effort and a fair share of skill will win him a place among his fellows that is not to be despised. Children are not slow to learn that cunning and underhandedness are no match for a straightforward honesty; and if good-feeling is to be preserved, any mean or unworthy act that may interfere with the general harmony meets at once with a universal reprobation that goes far to check the desire to secure unfair advantages. A fine manly spirit is engendered by healthy sports, and I venture to think that the more we can introduce these into India and imprint a love for them on the younger generation, so much the faster shall we progress in the work of civilization.

The inhabitants of Kooloo proper, Wuzeeri-Rupi, and Seoraj may, with some shades of difference in their characters, be regarded very much as one race. Mr. Trebeck's remark, at page 177 of Moorcroft's first volume, that "the people of Kooloo are stouter, and more active, and a finer race than any of the hill tribes we have yet seen, but they are savage and vindictive," may, with some modifications, be regarded as a not inapt description of the inhabitants of the Upper Beas valley, Wuzeeri-Rupi, and Seoraj; but it is unquestionable that the people of the two latter districts are superior in moral and intellectual ability to those in Kooloo proper. Like many of the hill races, the men of this part of the subdivision are not without a low cunning, which, as their past history plainly sets forth, degenerates under fitting auspices into downright treachery; and their indifference to truth, their want of a sense of responsibility, and their loose morality, stamp them as a class in whose favour not much can be advanced. Ignorant, lazy, deceitful, and dissolute, it is absolutely necessary to rule in Kooloo with a very firm hand, and a vigilance that must never be relaxed; and yet it would be unfair to say all the above without adding that those here under discussion are not without their good points. Though hating work, they labour uncommonly well when they see that orders are not to be trifled with, and their listless and sullen demeanour gives way to a cheerful alacrity, which comes strangely from those who hold anything in the way of unselfish exertion in downright detestation. The majority of the field-work is undertaken by the females, but no inconsiderable share of this falls to the men, who are certainly diligent agriculturists, though they may be lazy in other ways, and never are the women called on to aid in carriage of travellers' baggage, however heavy the pressure on the *Zemindars*. Again, among themselves there is a very neighbourly feeling; and though each *Zemindar's* fields must be planted out with the aid of others, a demand for payment for the services rendered is never heard of. In their dealings with one another they are generous, and not unfrequently entertain largely, and in their social relations there is but little wrangling or strife; and one may encamp, as I have more than once done, for days together within the precincts of a village and never hear an angry word or the least sign of a quarrel. Nor are they without a dim sense of gratitude, for in return for medicines and little acts of kindness I have had one or two instances brought to my notice of the recipients bringing their offerings of potatoes or honey, for which payment has been stoutly refused. On the whole, I am inclined to think that their faults are the result of a neglected education and a most imperfect civilization, to which the light of intelligence and refinement can hardly yet be said to have penetrated.

The women, as a rule, are soft and gentle in manner, with a shy and modest demeanour which is very winning; and it is but seldom that the female voice in Kooloo is heard in the tones of angry remonstrance or wordy dispute. It can be urged against them that they hold the marriage tie in very little regard; but, treated as they are by the males, at whose disposal they completely are, one can hardly be surprised at the levity of the wife; more open and frank in their manner than the men, to whom they are certainly equal in *physique* and superior in character, they, unlike their weaker sisters in the plains, resent oppression and ill-usage, and do not hesitate to act as they please, in defiance of relations and friends, when either their better feelings are outraged or they form a real attachment. With the Kooloo woman chastity has never been a strong point, and it is but too true that the ideas of both sexes with regard to the sacredness of the marriage-tie are not in accord with the views of more cultivated races. But the standard which may fittingly be adopted elsewhere cannot be applied in Kooloo, where ancient custom and intense ignorance have long been at work blunting all the finer susceptibilities; there is, however, an entire absence of that unbounded profligacy which is such a disgrace to every Christian country and city; and though in Kooloo continency is a virtue more honoured in the breach than in the observance, it cannot be charged to the erring that they stray from flagitious wilfulness or the greedy desire for gain.

The Lahoulees are shrewd and sharp traders, with far more intelligence and desire for knowledge than have the people of Kooloo. They are indifferent and most careless husbandmen, nor can it be urged in their behalf that they make the most of the advantages they have; and yearly, from sheer laziness, they neglect to make proper provision for their cattle, which in the long winter die in numbers, simply for want of the fodder that the commonest care in the summer would have secured to them. In their social relations with each other there is a good deal of the feudal feeling, and a kindly tone pervades all ranks. As a class, however, the Lahoulees are no more to be trusted than are the men of Kooloo, and their constant deceit and evasive practices have had a most serious effect in retarding the construction of the roads in Lahoul, which are, in truth, for their own benefit; and directly European supervision is removed from the works going on in the valley, nearly every man deserts his post, nor can any reliance be placed on the pretended goodwill of the leading *Thakoors*, who take no pains to secure the completion of the lines of communication which must result in very great gain to their own people. Rudeness or insolence to travellers is, I think I may say, almost unknown in Lahoul, and any supplies the natives have are given cheerfully on demand; and in this respect there is a favourable contrast to the state of things in Kooloo, where, unless the civil authorities are ever on the alert, the traveller might starve before the *Zemindar* would stir to assist him. Though in some respects improvident, the Lahoulee cannot be termed lazy, for nearly every family embarks in some small mercantile venture, and the people are constantly travelling about with their wares; and the practical wisdom of the majority is evidenced by their quitting their own dreary and inhospitable country for Kooloo when the winter sets in. The women are cheerful, merry, and hard-working, and spend much of their time in blanket-weaving, the construction of straw shoes, or in farm duties.

The Spiti peasant is good-natured, cheerful, and sociable, always ready to oblige, and industrious both as an agriculturist and an artisan. Dr. J. G. Gerard, in referring to the men of this valley, says, "they are black, greasy, and imbecile, without any noble qualities whatever;" but this traveller had only just before recorded, that he had been treated while in the country "with friendship and hospitality, unaccompanied by that savage feeling which protects a traveller as a guest and betrays him beyond the threshold of his sanctuary." The latter estimate is by far the truer one of the two. The Spiti *Zemindar* is not black, nor is he an imbecile; for if he were the latter, he would not be in a position to show the excellence he exhibits in his home manufactures. And some credit, too, must be allowed to a people who, far away from civilization, and knowing no tongue but Thibetan, are yet orderly and quiet in their behaviour, kindly and affectionate in all domestic relations, and never either obtrusive or impertinent to strangers. For my own part, I consider that, as a race, they are superior in many respects to the people of either Kooloo or Lahoul. They are very fond of their own country, and are never happy when away from it; they are excellent and most faithful guides in all the dangerous passes; they are not avaricious or greedy for money, and they are obedient subjects, who give no trouble, and carry out all orders with a promptitude that is commendable, and that might with advantage be followed in other parts of the subdivision. Each village community lives in peace and good-fellowship, for disputes are almost unknown; and I am inclined to regard the Spiti people as a singularly amiable and pleasing race, from whom the traveller, however much he may dislike the terrible monotony of their stony valley, will part with a feeling of kindly regret. Egerton, in speaking of the Spiti women, says, "Although they are as plain as low foreheads, little slanting eyes, and high cheek-bones can make them, although they are horribly dirty, yet their frank sociability, their cheerfulness and love of fun, the appreciation of a joke and ready repartee, their pleasant good-humoured voices and clear merry laugh, are (especially after a long residence in the land of female seclusion) extremely pleasing and refreshing."

Throughout Kooloo polygamy is the rule; but in parts of Seoraj it is not uncommon for two or more brothers to have one wife between them. When there is also a common property in goods, Mr. Lyall, in his Census Report for 1868, says, "in one house you may find three brothers with one wife, and in the next three brothers with four wives, all alike in common; in the adjoining house there will be an only son with four wives to himself. It is a matter of means and of land; a large farm requires several women to look after it." The system of polyandry appears, however, to be dying out in Kooloo, and is not regarded with favour. The women, too, unlike their Mormon sisters, object to the custom of polygamy; and for a husband to take to himself another wife is frequently a sure means of losing the one he has already. In Lahoul polyandry prevails extensively, one wife belonging generally to a family of brothers; but here, again, in some parts of the country, brothers prefer to have separate wives, and nearly all the men in the higher class are polygamists. Captain Hay mentions in his report on Spiti, that polyandry was in full force in that valley; but this is incorrect, and the people deny that it has any existence.

## CHAPTER IX.

**Local Trade in the Subdivision.—Lahoul, Spiti, and Kooloo Trade considered.—Measurements.—Handicrafts and Minor Products in the three Valleys. —Silversmiths, Carpentering, Weaving, Masons, Leather-workers, Pottery, Tanning, Basket-making, Rope-making, Paper-making, Oils, Dyes, Thatching, Slating, and Shingling.—Sculpture and Painting — General Geological Features.—Mineral Wealth.**

NEITHER in Kooloo, Lahoul, nor Spiti is the local trade extensive, for the inhabitants of each valley are essentially an agricultural people. The Kooloo *Zemindar* is too lazy and effete to trouble himself with the chance of gain in trafficking; and if the men of Lahoul or Spiti may be said to engage in mercantile transactions, these are but of small value, and the sphere of their operations very limited, for in no case do the people of the subdivision ever leave "the hills" with the wares they have for disposal. But commercial operations of a necessity do exist, and perhaps the most active and enterprising of the petty merchants are to be found in Lahoul, from whence every year a number of *Zemindars* pass into Kooloo, driving before them flocks of sheep and goats laden with borax purchased in Ladakh, or other stores of country produce, such as wool and *puttoo.*

The chief exports from Lahoul are borax, *pushmeena,* wool, spices, and dried fruits; but all these are procured in other countries, and cannot be deemed special home products.

The imports are brass and copper vessels, sugar, wheat, rice, and tobacco from Kooloo, apricots in the shape of dried fruit from Baltee, and, in addition, pepper, ginger, turmeric, garlic, and onions, that all come from the Kooloo side. The greater part of the population of Lahoul migrate as the autumn sets in, and squat in various parts of the Kooloo valley, returning in the spring to their homes laden with supplies, either for sale in Ladakh or home consumption.

The wants of the Spiti *Zemindar* are few,

and he does not greatly care about leaving his valley; occasionally, however, parties of men set off for Ladakh, Bussahir, and Kooloo, and there dispose of their wares, receiving payment in either money or kind.

The exports from Spiti are cereals, manufactured cloth, half-bred yâks, and yâks' tails; and the imports into Spiti consist of salt, madder, tobacco, tea from Lhassa, sheep's wool, turquoises, amber, waterpails, and other wooden vessels from Kunawur, coarse cloth, dyeing drugs, soda and yeast from Ladakh, and iron from Mundee and Kunawur. For grain they get an equal weight in salt, and for three *lacs*, or thirty-six seers of barley, eight *kurrees* (from twelve to sixteen seers) of wool is given. This wool is obtained from the people of Changthang and Chumurti, and what is over is sometimes disposed of in Bussahir or Kooloo. The Changthang sheep are a fine breed, and for one of these five *lacs* of grain (or sixty pucka seers) is the usual price. A considerable quantity of the grain is exported to Bussahir, with a part of the imported salt, rupees, iron, and tobacco being taken in exchange; and, again, some of this iron finds its way into Ladakh. The selling price of grain in Spiti is two and a half to three *lacs* of barley and two *lacs* of wheat for the rupee.

The Kooloo *Zemindar* cannot be termed a trader at all; he must be regarded more in the light of a farmer, who disposes by retail and wholesale of the produce of his lands. His rice he sells to the Lahoulees, and much of his wheat goes in the same direction, but purchasers for this last commodity are also found in the plains. His opium crop is taken off his hands entirely by traders from the Punjab and the adjoining hill states, and his tobacco, grown principally in the Upper valley, he retains for home consumption chiefly, but no inconsiderable portion of this finds its way to Lahoul and Spiti, Seoraj, and the states near Simla. Kooloo honey, which is extremely palatable, is exported to some extent, almost every house having its hives, the out-turn from which is generally considerable. Tea is not consumed by the people of the valley; it is nearly all exported to the plains. There is a small trade in blankets, which, towards Seoraj and Wuzeeri-Rupi, are of good quality; but these are mostly disposed of to visitors and resident shopkeepers, the price varying from Rs. 2 4 0 to Rs. 5 0 0.

Sheep are annually sold in large numbers, to agents who come from Simla, and fetch on an average over four shillings apiece; but flocks are kept not so much for sale as for home consumption, the flesh being much relished by the *Zemindars*, while the wool is turned to account in the construction of clothes.

A considerable quantity of borax comes down annually from Ladakh *viâ* Spiti and Lahoul, but this, as does all the trade from Ladakh and Eastern Turkistan, passes into the hands of foreign traders. Brass and copper cooking-pots are imported from the Punjab, as are salt and iron from Mundee, and spices and cottons from Hindoostan.

The agrarian measure in Kooloo and

Lahoul is by *bhars* and *pathas*, sixteen *pathas* going to one *bhar*. One *patha* is equal to ninety-five square yards, and one *bhar* to 1,520 square yards, which would give three *bhars* and three *pathas* in the statute acre of 4,840 square yards. In certain parts of Kooloo there is another description of measurement by *kansees*, four of these going to the *bhar*, the *kansee* being 380 square yards.

In Spiti the agrarian measure is by the *bhar* and *patha*, and also by the *lac*, thirty-two kutcha seers or twelve pucka seers going to the *lac*.

The linear measure differs considerably in various localities. Throughout the sub-division cloth is sold by the *hath* of about one foot eight inches in length, but the dimensions of the *hath* are not always the same.

In Kooloo and Lahoul the *seer* and *maund* are the same as in Hindoostan, but there are other measures in common use that are peculiar to particular tracts, such as the *buttee*, which is two *seers*. In Spiti the *seer* is but thirty-two *tolahs* instead of eighty, as in Hindoostan, and, according to Captain Hay, the people "have a measure called a *manee* or *thee*, which is a small wooden cup: this is of two sizes, the one used for buying, called *chagreh*, holding twenty-nine pounds' weight of grain; and the other, by which they sell, called *googreh*, which only holds twenty-one pounds' weight."

The cleverest handicraftsmen in the sub-division are to be found in Spiti, where some excellent blacksmith's work is to be obtained; the steel bits, buckles, and stirrups being specially worthy of note, as are the straight fluted steel pipes, occasionally ornamented with gold, the engraved steel cases for pens, and the brass and copper ink-bottles. *Chuck-muks*, or strike-lights, are also made in Spiti, but a better variety of these comes from Bussahir. The iron implements used in agriculture are all made in the valley. In Kooloo, Lahoul, and Spiti workers in iron are numerous, but they are, for the most part, rude craftsmen, all bolts and locks having to be procured ready made from the plains; and even the trade of shoeing horses is quite in the hands of the Kangra blacksmiths.

There are a few silversmiths in Kooloo, who can work up the common description of ornaments worn by the people, and men equally good are to be found in Lahoul and Spiti, who can execute with neatness the particular sort of jewellery most in request.

The art of carpentering is quite in its infancy throughout the entire subdivision. The rougher varieties of woodwork are of course carried on, but, with the wretched tools the people have, anything approaching to a neat style can never be secured. It is only within a few years that saws have been introduced into one part of Kooloo, *i. e.* the Upper Beas valley, and their use is, even now, extremely limited. In many of the houses there is a good deal of rude carving, and in the temples there are some specimens of a better order, and, under proper instruction, and with good implements, it is probable the people would somewhat improve·; at present, however, they do all they have to do in a very slovenly manner, and all finished work has to be given over to carpenters from Kangra. In the formation of *sungha* bridges the Kooloo *Zemindar* is particularly expert, and these structures are both strongly put together, and are very tasteful in appearance. Neither in Lahoul nor Spiti is there much opening for skill in woodwork, as timber in both these districts is so scanty, but some samples of carving which I have seen would point to a more natural talent for this art than is to be found in Kooloo.

In Kooloo the men alone do the weaving, whereas in Lahoul and Spiti this is undertaken by both sexes. The best blankets in Kooloo come from Seoraj and Wuzeeri-Rupi, those from the Upper Beas valley being much poorer in quality, and consequently much cheaper. The colours of the plaids are very varied, a uniform grey or deep brown, ornamented with running bars of variegated tints, being the general style; but it is not uncommon to see checks of black and white. The entire dress of the people in each part of the subdivision is home-made, and it is customary for each man to carry about with him his ball of wool and spindle, at which he works whenever he has nothing else to occupy his spare moments. The Spiti cloth is particularly good, and is of several descriptions. The strongest and thickest is made in long, narrow lengths, furred or plushed on one side, and is very durable and wonderfully cheap; another sort is rather finer than the above, and more expensive; and a third variety, woven from goat's hair, is equally good, and is much in demand with European residents in Kooloo. The products of Spiti in this particular are certainly superior to those either of Lahoul or Kooloo. In page 70 of Moorcroft's second volume, it is recorded that "2,752 pieces of cloth are annually fabricated in Spiti, of which 1,600 are used in home consumption, and the rest exported to the extent of 13,140 yards." This was written in 1820, and I should not imagine the manufacture had at all retrograded. In Lahoul an excellent thick carpeting is made of goat's hair; this is very cheap, but its weight tells against its ever growing much in public favour.

The masons throughout the entire sub-division have, as yet, only acquired the elements of their trade; they are able to run up the houses of the peasantry, but anything else is quite beyond their power.

The shoes worn in Kooloo, Lahoul, and Spiti are exported from the plains, but the Spiti winter boots are made by the leather-workers in Spiti, who are also good hands at saddlery. Sheepskins, with the wool on, are prepared very skilfully in Spiti and Lahoul, but this branch of the trade finds no existence in Kooloo; though there, as in the other two districts, nearly every household has its store of prepared sheep or goat skins, which are sewn up and converted into bags for the conveyance of grain.

Ordinary repairs in leather can be executed in most parts of the subdivision.

The potter's art is but little followed anywhere, nothing but a few simple vessels for holding water being ever attempted. Tanning, I may say, is unknown. Baskets are made everywhere; they are termed *kiltas* in Kooloo, and are strong and neat in appearance; in Spiti they are shorter and broader than in Kooloo. Smaller baskets for holding wool are also constructed.

Ropes are made from goat's hair, and of a stouter description from the twigs of the willow or birch, these last being chiefly utilized in the formation of *jhula* bridges; in Lahoul a very excellent rope is woven from the *Desmodium*, the long stems of which are twisted together into an exceedingly enduring cable.

The ignorance of the people throughout Kooloo renders the preparation of paper a useless work, and, if occasion require, the necessary supply can always be had at Sooltanpore from the native shopkeepers.

The soft bark of the birch, which has many linings, is, however, utilized for wrapping up articles; and in Lahoul this same bark is the substitute for paper, though this substance is not unfrequently made from a *Desmodium*, which, by all accounts, appears to form a suitable material for writing purposes. Egerton mentions that a paper is manufactured in Spiti from a kind of grass that grows wild in the Peen valley, and by Manee village, below Dhunkur; and Captain Hay, in his report on Spiti, alludes to the fact that 132 *shoogoes* of paper (equal to 600 Hindoostani *takhtas*) were paid in 1839 as part of the Spiti tribute to the ruler of Ladakh. It is probable that this paper was made from the grass above referred to.

In Kooloo a very fine oil is made from the poppy-seed, as also from the bruised kernels of apricots and peaches, from mustard, and from various other grain-bearing weeds. Each *Zemindar* prepares a sufficient supply for his household wants, but not enough for sale, and it therefore is not easy for the

European residents to obtain oil in any large quantities. In Lahoul all the oil used for lighting is imported, but a vegetable oil is also expressed, to a very limited extent, says Aitcheson, from a common weed of the valley, the *Impatiens tingens;* this, however, is only used for polishing cups and such-like wooden vessels. In Spiti oil is made exclusively from mustard.

In Spiti several dyes are used. "The red dye employed is madder, imported *viâ* Kangra, and for yellow an indigenous root, called *myaloo.* Before applying these dyes the cloth is steeped in a mordant, for which is used a kind of earth, probably lime in some form or other, and which is everywhere found in Spiti." (Egerton.) In Lahoul there are no dyers, the whole of the trade being in the hands of men from Kooloo, who occasionally pass through the valley; Aitcheson, however, mentions two plants, the *Rubia cordifolia* and *Polygonum tortuosum,* which both yield a yellow dye. In Kooloo a great variety of tints are produced by the dyer's art, but green is a colour which the people have very seldom succeeded in obtaining. The most vivid blues, reds, and yellows are to be met with everywhere, with the gradations from grey to burnt sienna, madder, and black.

Thatching is not practised in either Spiti or Lahoul, the roofs of houses in these parts of the subdivision being nearly all flat; in Lahoul, however, there are one or two houses provided with shingled or timbered roofs. In Kooloo slates, planks, and thatch are all used, and the roofs are often very neatly and even artistically laid. Where a slaty formation is near at hand, full advantage is taken of its propinquity, in other cases logs of *deodar* being used. Thatching with grass, except in the dwellings of the poorer classes, is but seldom resorted to. In the Upper Beas valley slating and shingling are common, but the villages on the right bank of the Beas, from Sooltanpore to below Bajoura; have all flat earthen roofs; in Wuzeeri-Rupi and Seoraj timber is not much

17

used for roofing purposes, slate being preferred.

Whatever art might have been in ancient days in Kooloo, it has now certainly fallen into a deplorably low state. There are many evidences that sculpture and wood-carving were once generally cultivated, and there are a few instances which evince considerable skill both in the manipulation and pose of the figures to be seen in the numerous temples. The trade of the sculptor has now, however, quite died out. In Lahoul and Spiti carving in stone never appears to have been followed as a profession; but while in Kooloo there are no signs that painting was ever regarded with favour, in Spiti and Lahoul it is still the custom to decorate the monasteries with large pictures in colours. In the *lamasery* of Shaeshorgh, above Kielung, in Lahoul, the whole of the walls of the oratory are completely covered with paintings, which are, I think, superior to what is ever seen in Hindoo temples; and in Moorcroft's second volume, in the portion referring to Spiti, there is a description given of a very clever statue of Sankya Muni in woodwork, which was both well carved and handsomely gilt and painted. The Spiti monasteries are also decorated with coloured figures, but it may be that both in Lahoul and Spiti these are executed by foreign artists; and Egerton, in alluding to the wooden sculptures at Tabo, in Spiti, appears also to incline to this belief.

The geological formation of Kooloo is "composed of Silurian rocks, sandstone, shales, clay-slate, micaceous and quartzose schists, with unusually numerous quartz lodes, most of which are highly metalliferous." * With regard to Spiti, Captain Hay reported that the formation belonged to the secondary period; "in fact," he says, "Spiti may be described generally as being of various kinds of lime and sandstone, with a few slates, shales, and conglomerates." Much the same general features may be observed in Lahoul;

* "Minerals of India," by J. Calvert.

but of the geology of this last part of the subdivision I have never been able to learn much.

Kooloo appears to be particularly rich in mineral wealth, but none of the lodes have been regularly worked of late years. In Wuzeeri-Rupi there are said to be undoubted evidences of veins of silver, copper, and lead; and last year (1869) the contract for the working of the mines in this tract of country was given by the Jaghirdar, with the consent of Government, to Mr. John Calvert; but up to date nothing very much has been effected. Various lodes have been discovered in different parts of the Upper Beas valley, which would all presumably be worth working; and traces of a very pure white crystal and antimony have been met with near Juggutsookh and in the Upper Chundra valley. It was surmised by Captain Hay that there must be rock-salt in Spiti, as the water in the Spiti river is for several miles above Dhunkur quite saline in flavour, and it is not unlikely that this valuable mineral does exist in that valley. The people of Spiti, it is true, do not profess to be aware of there being salt in their country; but no experiments have apparently ever been made, and there is a natural reluctance to give any inkling as to ores, for the people believe the burden of working these will be cast upon them. Slate of a very fair quality is obtainable all throughout Kooloo, the better descriptions being found near Sooltanpore and at Muling village, in Lahoul; and for roofing, as before stated, slates are extensively used in Kooloo, but not at all in Lahoul, the only exception being in the case of the Moravian mission-house at Kielung. The Lahoul slate has been pronounced to be the best in the subdivision, it being of a deep-blue colour, and splitting up into broad and sufficiently long and even sheets.

In Wuzeeri-Rupi, the copper-mines at Pillan, and the salt which is reported to exist at Barogi, are said to have been worked in the time of Rajah Mann Sing, and the Sikhs, it is known, attempted to utilize some mines in the same tract, which are believed to be rich in silver ore. It can hardly be doubted that the mineral wealth of Kooloo is enormous, and that as yet no fair attempts have been made to develop this; but, separated as the country is from all markets, it is doubtful whether any scheme for working the many valuable mines will ever be a paying transaction, the difficulty in procuring labour and the cost of transport being so very heavy.

## CHAPTER X.

**Health of the People.—Statistics of the Helpless Classes. —Dispensary.—Food and Beverages in Kooloo, Lahoul, and Spiti.—Tobacco.**

PROBABLY owing to their fine dry climate, Spiti and Lahoul are particularly free from most of the maladies that flesh is heir to; but skin diseases sometimes appear, and smallpox is said to have raged in Spiti some years ago. All throughout Kooloo, fever towards the autumn becomes rife; but, as far as I have been able to ascertain, the disease is not one positively dangerous to life, although it is very prostrating in its effects, and extremely difficult to shake off. A form of gastritis is also not uncommon, this being mainly superinduced by the great quantities of unripe fruit, poppy-seeds, and apricot and peach kernels, which are so largely consumed. Bronchocele, scrofula, and goitre are all but too prevalent, and occasionally smallpox has added its heavy quota to the death-average. At the census of 1868 the following statistics were published :—

| | | | |
|---|---|---|---|
| No. of Blind in Kooloo | | ... | 368 |
| „ | Deaf | ... ... | 172 |
| „ | Dumb | ... ... | 237 |
| „ | Lepers | ... ... | 151 |
| „ | Insane | ... ... | 6 |

which gives a total of 934 incapables in a population of over 98,000 souls; but I am convinced that the above figures do not fully represent the numbers of the afflicted.

There is but one dispensary in the sub-division, and that is at Sooltanpore; so for all practical purposes it may be said the greater proportion of the three districts is almost destitute of medical aid. It is true that the Rev. Messrs. Rechler and Heyde in Lahoul, the Rev. Mr. Carleton at Plach, and Mr. Miniken, the manager of the Kooloo Tea Company, in the lower part of the Beas valley, all afford a great deal of reliefin their own immediate neighbourhoods, and have been the means of saving many lives and lessening much suffering; but the great mass of the people are left without any prospect of aid in case of sickness. When fever rages, as it often does in the autumn, the sufferers have for the most part to get on as they best can, trusting entirely to nature, for any reliable "advice" is quite out of the question at the distance they necessarily must be from either European residents or the Dispensary at Sooltanpore. It would be highly desirable could an English sub-assistant surgeon be placed in medical charge of Kooloo, for at present the medical staff in the valley is quite inadequate to the wants of the population.

There are in all some eighteen or twenty English residents in the valley every summer, and in the season at least fifty or sixty travellers pass through the country, and in case of any urgent need, it cannot be held that a native doctor would be likely to give much satisfaction. There are many very indigent persons in the valley, and when to these are added the nine hundred and odd who are blind, deaf, dumb, and paralyzed, it will be allowed that there is a great mass of misery, to cope with; but there is no "Poorhouse," nor any funds for keeping such an institution in working order. Mr. Knox, who was formerly Assistant-Commissioner in Kooloo, has in the handsomest manner promised Rs. 3,000 towards the Dispensary, and if to this could be added a poorhouse, provided by an equivalent Government grant, very considerable relief would result. Unfortunately, the head men in Kooloo are not to be trusted with the disposal of charitable donations that may be subscribed for the poorer classes; and I think the only plan would be to have a poorhouse as near to Nuggur as possible, where it would be under the constant observation of the Assistant-Commissioner in charge of the subdivision.

In Kooloo the people eat three times a day; the breakfast, called *kulār*, is at eight or nine A.M.; the dinner, *dopaharee* or *dhyan*, at one or two P.M.; and the *byalee*, or supper, at sunset. Those who are better off eat both the best descriptions of rice and flour; but the more general food of the *Zemindars* is made up of *sidhoo*, *pheemra*, or *kuppee*. *Sidhoo* is formed from *attah joa* or *mukkhi*, worked into thin cakes; *pheemra* is either *ghulla* or *sureara* (amaranth) and rice mixed together, or rice with a little *attah*, and such vegetable roots as are procurable; while *kuppee* is a concoction of rice and vegetables stewed. Unlike Hindoostanees, the Kooloo people put salt on their food when eating it, and not while it is being cooked: during the meal no fermented liquor is drunk, but at feasts and *melas* it is partaken of largely in the form of *loogree*. For drunkenness salt is used as a restorative.

*Loogree*, the pernicious drink of the people of the Upper Beas valley and Lahoul, is a fruitful source of illness. It is drunk in enormous quantities, the makers of the spirit being all Lahoulees, who may have settled in Kooloo. There are several sorts of *loogree*, but the best is made from honey and a variety of shrubs, to which conglomerate the name of *dhaellee* is given. The honey being placed in a large *ghurra*, the *dhaellee* (leaves, stem, and all) are flung in, water is added, and fire applied below, and kept burning for three days; on the first day a sort of condiment or yeast, termed *mundul*, being mixed with the mess. When the three days have expired, the *ghurra* is taken off the fire and put inside the house, blankets being placed over it to prevent any sudden change of atmosphere: a month after it has thus lain by, the liquor is ready for drinking.

A second sort of *loogree* is made from rice, the component parts being one piece of *pav* (Ladakh yeast) to every four *seers* of rice. Sixteen *seers* of rice being cooked, it is allowed to get cold, and then the yeast in the above proportions is broken up and inserted into the mess. The ensuing day the concoction is placed in a *ghurra*, into which a *seer* of water is poured, the mouth of the vessel being then securely fastened. In four or five days the contents of the *ghurra* are strained through a cloth, and the fluid that escapes is the *loogree.* In a third sort of *loogree* the recipe is something as follows:—To *chupatties*, or the paste from *attah*, are added the shrubs termed *dhaellee*, and water as desirable; the whole is then inserted in a caldron, which is kept closed for at least twelve days; but it is sometimes six months before the liquor is fit for drinking.

Neither in Wuzeeri-Rupi nor in Seoraj is any fermented liquor ever drunk, but tobacco is used all throughout the subdivision, except in one or two villages in the Surburri valley, where smoking has by long custom been discountenanced.

It would be a very good thing for the people of the Upper Beas valley and Lahoul, if some sound and cheap liquor could be introduced that might supersede *loogree.* There seems a natural eagerness on the part of the people to engage in deep drinking bouts, and the *loogree*-shop in the Upper Beas valley is about the one place where squabbling and fighting comes off. It is said, I know not with what truth, that opportunities are taken in these debauches, both in Kooloo and Lahoul, to pay off old scores, and I am afraid these suspicions are not altogether groundless. A revel is got up, to which the doomed man is invited; and while half stupid with the disgusting concoction called *loogree*, his enemy, as if accidentally, rolls him over the roof or verandah, and the people, to avoid getting themselves into trouble, send in the usual statement that so-and-so died from natural causes, and thus the whole matter is hushed up. I believe it would not be impolitic to pronounce the brewing of *loogree* altogether illicit; the people would only object to its prohibition in the event of no other liquor being procurable; and with the disappearance of *loogree*, some better and more innocuous spirit might easily be introduced, and sold under proper supervision.

Buckwheat is the principal staple of food in Lahoul, and from this two descriptions of flour are made; one called *drape*, of the raw grain, which is, when boiled with water, eaten as gruel; and the other termed *mukusu*, made of grain first boiled and then roasted. This *mukusu* flour, says Dr. Aitcheson, in his pamphlet on the *Flora* of Lahoul, is either formed into a species of girdle cake, or is mixed with *chang* in two proportions where there is but little of it; and dumplings thus formed are carried in travelling, or are converted into a gruel and drunk off on the spot. "Wheaten flour is eaten largely made into a sort of soup, with such vegetables as can be obtained, as, in spring, dandelions and other field weeds (in summer chiefly the leaves of the buckwheat); and this soup forms the chief morning meal. Rice-flour is used much in the same way as the wheaten by the poorer people" (Aitcheson); but the wealthier classes prefer it in the Ladakh fashion, mixed with apricots, sugar, and condiments, and boiled with butter: barley-flour is utilized in the same manner as is wheaten flour, and roasted barley is frequently eaten, but is regarded in the light of a delicacy. A large tap-root, called *ludut*, is, when dried, often converted into flour and mixed with barley or buckwheat; and, by way of luxury, cakes formed of dried apricots are much appreciated, and are always kept ready for visitors in the houses of the richer men.

Tea, cooked with clarified butter, is much in use among the higher classes: this is made into a thick mess, and, as a substitute, the poorer people infuse the leaves of the *Potentilla Inglisii*. *Chang*, very much the same as the Kooloo *loogree*, is made from rice and barley, the grain being boiled, and then squeezed by hand. *Chang*, like *loogree*, is a thick, dirty-looking fluid, with a most nauseous smell, and a taste that is detestable to those accustomed to European liquors: a species of *arrack* is also made from barley. The milk of the sheep, goat, and cow is also drunk by Lahoulees. The hybrid between the yak and the cow gives the best milk, from which first-class butter is made; buttermilk is also much esteemed, and is occasionally converted into a fermented beverage, by mixing it with a species of leaven made from roasted barley-meal. The Lahoulees will eat the flesh of almost any animal, whatever the cause of death may have been; but they have a great reluctance, except in special cases, to participate in the supposed crime of slaughtering anything.

In Spiti, the food in main use, says Hay, in his report on Spiti, consists of *suttoo*, made of wheat, barley, or peas; and Egerton states that the Spiti people have three meals a day. "First, in the morning, hot gruel, made from parched barley-meal, called *pho-loo:* a bit of meat is added, if they have it. Secondly, at midday, a huge lump of *suttoo* or parched barley-meal, kneaded into a tough dough, which is washed down with *chang*, butter-milk, or water, as the case may be. This seems a most uncomfortable meal in every respect. It is eaten in the fields, or on the road, or wherever a man happens to be, the mass of dough being carried about in the breast of the coat (next the skin of course, as no under garment is worn) until dinner-time. . . . The evening meal is gruel, as in the morning."

Tea in Spiti is prepared in the following manner: *—"The tea is placed in a pipkin, with a little cold water and some soda," and boiled; some hot water is then added, and the hot tea poured into the tea-churn; butter and milk being added, the whole is well churned, and served up with the froth on. The tea in use in Spiti is imported from Lhassa, and is only used by the better classes who can afford the luxury; the Indian teas are not liked by the people. Egerton gives the following description of *chang*-making. To a quantity of parched barley double the weight of water is added; to this "put in a pinch of dried yeast, called *phav*, about one drachm to ten pounds of malt, and leave it to ferment for two or three days." The yeast comes from Ladakh, and its composition is a secret.

Tobacco is smoked both in the *chillum*

* Egerton's "Tour in Spiti."

and also from the long steel pipe, which each Spiti Zemindar carries in his waistcloth, his pouch of tobacco being also fastened close to his *chuckmuk* or strike-light. The women in Spiti do not smoke.

## CHAPTER XI.

**Begar or Forced Labour.—Visitors to the Valley.—European Residents in the Subdivision.—Tours in the District.—Postal and Telegraphic Communications.**

THE system of *begar*, or forced labour, is one that may almost be termed peculiar to the hills. To a certain extent it certainly prevails throughout India; in the plains applying more to the requisitions of Government for beasts of burden and carts, while in the Himalayan ranges the demand extends to the compulsory service of the *Zemindars*. The custom is a very ancient one, and is to this day in full force in all hill states; but in these last the labour of the people is not paid for, though it is not unusual for the governing power to supply the workmen with rations while engaged in State service.

In Kooloo various efforts have been made

to limit the call on the agricultural population as much as possible, and last year, this subject having been duly considered, I drew out a series of rules that will be noticed below, and which received the sanction of the Government. There are many difficulties in taking up such a matter as this. The State has, by immemorial usage, the right to demand *begar* in the case of all Government works, and for the porterage of travellers' goods; and as long as the pressure was not severe, the *Zemindar* had but few just causes of complaint. As years passed, however, circumstances changed, the calls for *begar* for the construction of roads and public buildings became more frequent, and travellers, who were during the first period of our rule unknown in Kooloo, increased in numbers, and every year now sees a steady incursion of tourists, who pass either from the plains to Simla or towards Ladakh and Cashmere. It therefore became evident that the old arrangements were daily becoming more unsuitable, and in endeavouring to compass the difficulties that were so frequently being brought to the notice of the civil authorities, it was necessary to take into consideration the interests of the Government, the *Zemindar*, and the English traveller. Of the Government,—for without the aid of the people of the country, it would be simply impossible to carry on any State works; of the *Zemindar*,—for his services could not be constantly brought into requisition without great loss to himself; and of the traveller, —as, were *begar* to be suddenly done away with, all means of transit must have been at once put an end to. Now the Government had, by the terms of the settlement and by ancient custom, the power to call on the *Zemindars* for *begar;* but in dealing with the people, it was desirable to work as little as possible on the compulsory system; though, while every scope was given to the exercise of free and willing labour, the right to demand *begar* was held in reserve. The *Zemindar* regarded it as the natural order of things, when called on, to give his labour to the State, nor was he averse to the carriage of travellers' effects; but in all such cases it became advisable to fix with something like accuracy the amount of compensation for the services rendered. The traveller, passing through Kooloo, merely saw in his porters men who made their living by the carriage of goods, and was at a loss to understand why there was delay in obtaining his full complement of coolies, and demurred in too many cases to paying any sum in fair proportion to the toil the *begarees* had to undergo. It became then a positive duty so to fix the rates that the traveller should not be mulcted too heavily; and, at the same time, that the *Zemindar* should not be too much out of pocket by his enforced absence from his fields, and that the burden of *begar* should fall equally on the various *kothees*.

This burden had for long been very carelessly adjusted; and the rapid changes in the Assistant-Commissioners in charge of the subdivision prevented anything like a due weighing of the matter. At some stages *several kothees* supplied the regular quota of men; while at others, where the influx of travellers was infinitely heavier, the number of *begarees* available was far below what it should have been; and when the people complained of this, and, in addition, were able to point to the incontestable fact, that a *Zemindar*, on a sudden call for *begar*, had often to come from his village fifteen or sixteen miles distant, be kept waiting several days before it was the traveller's pleasure to proceed, be grudgingly paid his two or three annas (often receiving nothing), and then have to trudge home again; it can be perceived at once that, called away, as he bably was, just when his little patch of ground demanded constant care and attention, the services demanded of him were deemed an intolerable burden, for which the insignificant payment tendered could not, by any reasonable person, be held as a fitting compensation. Lists have, accordingly, been made out of all the stages in Kooloo, Lahoul, and most of those in Spiti, with the rates of porterage attached; the complement for each stage suppliable from each *kothee* was fixed, and the following rules for *begar* were sanctioned by Government:—

A. Government will demand no *begar* during *Jeth*, *Har*, *Asoj*, and *Kathuk* * for original works, unless the execution of such be an imperative necessity, and an attempt has been made to procure willing labour, and has failed.

B. Government during those four months will only call on the people to give *begar* for repairs of old roads, erection of sungha bridges, and of houses of refuge on passes.

C. During the rest of the year, if *begar* is required, an attempt will be made to procure willing labour before the *begar* system is enforced.

D. In all cases of *begar* for Government (unless for repairs of old roads), the labourers will be paid at regular wages, and lump sums will not be given to the *Negees* to distribute;

* The four Hindoo months, during which, in Kooloo, the main agricultural operations are carried on.

an exception to this ruling will be allowed, however, in erection of *sungha* bridges, which are best constructed on the lump-sum system.

E. *Begar* can only be called for through the civil authorities; the Forest Department, for instance, must make its own arrangements for labour; but in cases of sudden emergencies, such as fires, floods, &c., that Department will be entitled to *begar*.

F. *Begar* is to be supplied to travellers at rates payable according to a written scale.*

The entire redistribution of *kothees* that supplied *begar* in the Upper Beas valley was also taken in hand, and the arrangements arrived at will probably be found to answer, at any rate for the time being.

It was my earnest desire that Government should establish a mule train in Kooloo, but the suggestion was deemed premature; and a private contractor has been induced, on a consideration of an advance of Rs. 5,000, to

* *Vide* letter of Commissioner of Jullundur division to Deputy-Commissioner of Kangra, No. 827, of 21st March, 1870.

enter the field, and supply sixty mules for hire in Kooloo; and, doubtless, his advent in the valley will be of great assistance to traders and tourists, and will materially lessen the pressure on the *Zemindars*.

It might be imagined that the constant influx of visitors in Kooloo would be hailed by the people with satisfaction; but it is, in fact, exactly the contrary. The traveller who comes into the valley, as a rule, has quite enough money to spend, and is not unwilling to part with it freely; he desires to buy the blankets, the *puttoo*, the honey, and the other native products, and he is not averse to paying liberally for all supplies; but the Kooloo *Zemindar* does not care to sell anything, and throws every obstacle in the way of tourists obtaining even ordinary necessities. He has not the sense to see that it would be quite feasible for him to secure a handsome profit from these free-handed strangers; and unless actually compelled to do so, he will neither part with his sheep nor his fowls, and uses every artifice to escape the demand for milk, grass, or firewood. So indifferent is he to his own interest, that he prefers to allow the entire local trade to be monopolized by foreigners; and it is a curious fact well worthy of attention, that throughout all Kooloo there is not a single shopkeeper who is not either a native of Kangra, the neighbouring states, or the plains. At every camping-stage Bunniahs or grain-sellers are to be found; but none of these are Kooloo men, and therefore the money the traveller disburses cannot be said, in any way, to profit the inhabitants of the country.

Thus the Kooloo people prefer to see the wealth that should come to them pass into the hands of others; and ignorant, and desiring to remain so, they will neither learn nor allow their children to be taught; and as long as this state of things continues, the foreign shopkeepers must have the field to themselves. The arrangement at present is for the *Zemindars* of such and such a *kothee* to give *begar* to the Bunniah, who has all his supplies of *attah*, &c., brought in for nothing to his shop; and thus the lucky tradesman has his carriage free, a house given him to live in, and no other occupation but to make money as fast as he can. Probably in no part of India is the petty tradesman so well off as he is in Kooloo; and well off he must remain till the people of the country will shake off their sloth and learn to deal for themselves.

There is in Kooloo a most unaccountable reluctance to sell produce; and it is incorrect to assert, as some do, that a fair price would always insure sales, for this aphorism does not apply to Kooloo at all. The *Zemindar* may have a dozen spare plaids in his house, and far more sheep and fowls than he cares about keeping, but not one article will he dispose of, even when such is urgently required, unless he feels the pressure of the authorities upon him. This pressure should doubtless be exerted as seldom as possible and only on very necessary occasions; but in certain cases it is indispensable for the Assistant Commissioner to come to the relief of travellers. Not merely, either, is there trouble in procuring ordinary necessities for Europeans, for native servants, if sent alone through the valley, can only with infinite difficulty obtain subsistence.

There are not many European residents in the subdivision,—in Spiti there are none at all; but in Kielung, in Lahoul, there has been for many years a branch of the Moravian mission. At present this mission is represented by the Rev. Messrs. Rechler and Heyde, who, with their families, have long resided in the well-built and substantial mansion that they themselves erected, and which is fitted up throughout quite in the German style. A large lower apartment is reserved for the chapel, and here every Sunday services are held, the one in the morning being in Thibetan for the benefit of such Lahoulees and Ladakhees who may care to attend. As far as conversions go, the success of the mission in this remote part of the world has not been very pronounced; but the influence of these good men is working much to the advantage of the people around, who, although they will not embrace the new creed taught, yet appreciate the unselfishness of those who have thus exiled themselves from their country, and resort to them for advice and assistance both in cases of sickness and adverse circumstances. Nor must it ever be forgotten that it is an immense advantage, having the watchful eye of Europeans in a district so far from all authority. If the leading men oppress the poorer people, the latter at once repair to the missionaries, and if injustice is perpetrated, the lowest classes know it will be only necessary to represent their case for steps to be taken to set wrong right; and in not a few instances have important matters, which would otherwise have quite escaped observation, been brought to the notice of the Assistant-Commissioner of Kooloo by either Mr. Rechler or Mr. Heyde. These gentlemen give their gratuitous services to the cause of education in the Government school at Kielung, and I may say, it is *entirely owing* to their exertions that the pupils have got on so well as they have. Their supervision of Government works, too, such as construction of serais, bridges, and roads, has been most ungrudgingly given, and merits the very warmest thanks of the Government, for it has in truth been invaluable. In the Mission-house at Kielung an apartment is set aside as a guest-room, and all who have passed through Lahoul can bear testimony to the genuine kindness and generous hospitality of the Moravian missionaries; and I do not hesitate to assert that, were they to quit Lahoul, their departure would be a great misfortune for that tract of country.

In Kooloo, which rejoices in a more equable climate than does Lahoul, there are several European residents. The Kooloo Tea Company have tea-gardens at Nuggur and Raesun, in the Upper Beas valley, and another still larger one at Bajoura, below Sooltanpore. Their resident manager, Mr. Miniken, resides with his family at either Raesun or Bajoura, and he, as do other

Europeans in the valley, affords considerable assistance to the people in all cases of illness. The Rev. Mr. Carleton has for many summers located himself in Seoraj, and his knowledge of medicine has very much benefitted those in the vicinity of his house, a small building at Plach, in Seoraj, placed at the disposal of his mission by Mr. Knox, the owner.

Captain Lee, a retired officer of H.M. 35th Foot, has lately settled in a very comfortable house he has himself built at Bundrole, about seven miles to the north of Sooltanpore, and General Conynghame owns a bungalow at Juggutsookh (some fifteen miles higher up the valley), which is placed under charge of the manager of the Kooloo Tea Company. The Forest department has also its representatives in Kooloo. Mr. Duff, the Assistant-Conservator of the Beas Forest division, has his headquarters at Menalee, very near the Rohtung Pass, there being, beside his house in that place a small Government bungalow, built for the use of the Assistant-Commissioner of Kooloo. Captain Greig, late of the 93rd Highlanders, also owns a small house at Dobee, on the right bank of the Beas, ten miles north of Sooltanpore.

There are many enjoyable tours to be had in this subdivision. The country from Bajoura downwards over the Busloh Pass towards Nirmand, and to Simla by the Jalouri Pass, is not without interest; but except actually close to the passes, the scenery in this part of the district is not much worthy of notice. The Parbuttee valley in Wuzeeri-Rupi is exceedingly beautiful, and a visit to the hot springs at Manikurn would well repay the traveller in search of the grand and picturesque; and this tour can be extended by crossing over the Kundee and Malauna Passes to Nuggur, in the Upper Beas valley, the village of Malauna, with its curious people, being one of the special objects of interest in Kooloo. The whole upward course of the Beas on either bank is rich in glimpses of lofty mountain and spreading forest, and perhaps no valley in India can be held to exceed Kooloo proper in the wondrous beauty of the views obtainable in every direction. Passing into Lahoul, we come to a region of barren desolation, broken, however, by pleasant gleams of rich cultivation and villages scattered over the swelling uplands; and, finally, Spiti, with its bare and solemn hills, and utter absence of all arboriculture, has features of its own which are very striking and impressive.

The only regular postal town in Kooloo is Sooltanpore, where a Deputy Post-master holds his office. The mail bags are sent to Kooloo, *viâ* the Bubboo Pass, from Palumpore, and *vice versâ*, during the summer months; but in the winter, as the above road is closed in places by snow, the runners take the old line by the Bajoura Pass, which necessitates a lengthier *détour*. During the summer there is regular postal communication kept up with Kielung, in Lahoul, where the schoolmaster officiates as Deputy Post-master as long as there is work to be done. The bags leave Sooltanpore thrice a week for

Kielung, and are returned in a similar order. This year a post has been laid out from Kielung to Leh, but it has worked in a very unsatisfactory manner. The arrangements were under the care of the *Negee* of Lahoul, whose business it was to supply runners for the entire line. Dr. Cayley,* however, relieved the *Negee* of a good deal of the work, and had Ladakh runners laid from the Ladakh side of the Bara Lacha Pass up to Leh; but very little improvement resulted from this change, and the experiment so far must be regarded as a failure.

There is no telegraphic communication in the subdivision.

* In 1870 Dr. Cayley was British Agent at Leh, the chief town of Ladakh.

## CHAPTER XII.

**Education in Kooloo, Lahoul, and Spiti. — Ignorance of the Masses, with resulting Evils. — Marriage Customs.**

THROUGHOUT the subdivision education is very backward. Efforts have, however, of late been made to improve this state of things; and in 1869, Nathoo Ram, a student from the Lahore College, was appointed Chief Mohurrir of Kooloo, and has been very zealous in inducing the Zemindars to send their sons to school, and instilling a desire for education into the masses. There are now schools in Kooloo at Sooltanpore, Plach, Nirmand, Dwarra, Nuggur, and Juggutsookh, all of which have a fair attendance of pupils, who are taught Persian, Oordoo, geography, history, and arithmetic. The Sooltanpore school is the largest of all these, and has on its list some sixty boys; nor is the attendance at the Plach school much smaller. Mr. Knox, who was formerly Assistant-Commissioner of Kooloo, gives a donation of twenty-five rupees *per mensem* to the Sooltanpore school. In Lahoul the only Government school is the one at Kielung, where the schoolmaster also takes up the duties of post-master. Very great progress has been made in this institution, in which are taught Oordoo and Thibetan, besides the other ordinary branches of study. When I visited the Kielung school in 1869 there were forty-eight boys present, and I was enabled to ascertain for myself what a very satisfactory advance had been made. The credit for this state of things is due to the Rev. Messrs. Heyde and Rechler, the missionaries at Kielung, who daily devote much time to the tuition of the boys, and are deeply interested in their being properly instructed. In Spiti, as in Lahoul, many of the people can read and write Thibetan, but very few of the inhabitants understand Oordoo. It was to remedy this state of affairs that Mr. Forsyth, then Commissioner of Jullundur (in 1867), ordered two boys from each of the five *kothees* in Spiti to be in regular attendance at Kielung; and it has been the rule since for these Spiti lads to be taught there. There is, in my opinion, more intelligence, and I may add cleverness, in the Spiti boys than are exhibited in the children of either Kooloo or Lahoul. Probably in time teachers from the Kielung school may be drafted off into Spiti, for it cannot be expected that any Hindustani would take up his residence in Spiti as a teacher, or would, if there and left all to himself, do much for the spread of education.

In Kooloo the ignorance of the people is dense, very few of even the better classes being able to read or write, and this is partly to be accounted for by the fact of there having been no royal court for so many years in Kooloo. When the country was ruled by its native chiefs, it was absolutely indispensable to have not only about the Rajah, but in every *kothee*, men who could read and write, for without such how could the collections in money or grain be properly checked? When our rule superseded that of the Sikhs, officials from Kangra were sent up for limited periods, and after a two or three years' stay were relieved by others; and it was by these men, whether as tehsildars, policemen, writers, or chuprassies, that the whole business of the country was carried on. For the Kooloo people to learn was useless, as appointments were always made from below, and the Kangra officials took up every petty place that might otherwise have been granted to an inhabitant of the country. Latterly, as the men of Kooloo have shown themselves even tolerably fit, I have placed them in all minor offices, and I am in hopes that ere long, with the proficiency many of them are making in the schools, it may be possible to find men in the valley who may safely be nominated to fill more important posts. But the very ignorant state of the people has affected their condition and their customs in many ways, as is evinced in the relations of the sexes, as I shall now propose to show.

The Kooloo Zemindar, if not betrothed as a child, when he wants to secure a wife visits a family where there are daughters, and expresses a desire to marry one of the girls, whose willingness to the proposed arrangement is seldom asked or considered. Generally speaking, the bridegroom agrees to give thirty or forty rupees to the father of the bride; and although it is always denied, there is but little doubt that the taking a wife is a mere piece of barter; the daughter being disposed of to some eligible swain, who, in recompense for the girl's services in the homestead, pays so much down for the privilege of securing her field-labour. Such marriages, as can be fancied, but seldom turn out happily; the wife has been brought up in an atmosphere of intrigue and domestic infidelity, has seen both her parents more than indifferent to the marriage-tie, and even if at first inclined to a quiet and regular life, she is either tempted astray in the numerous drunken feasts at the *melas*, or, deserted by her husband, and outraged by his repeated intrigues, at last throws off restraint, and follows that course of conduct which best pleases her, being tolerably certain she will escape punishment even if her guilt be discovered; for it seldom happens the injured husband has any desire to see his wife punished, as her confinement to prison would cause the loss of her labour on his farm. Nor has he any reluctance to take back his wife, whatever her profligacy may have been; he forgives, for he feels that if he does not condone her offence, it will simply result in his having to buy another woman, who may in all probability act just as did the last.

Thus the immunity of the woman from punishment—for the infidelity of the wife is too widespread to insure her ever being a subject of scorn to her own sex—and the immorality and licentiousness of the men, have tended to reduce the moral tone in Kooloo to a very low depth; nor are lapses of virtue or a state of concubinage looked upon with disapproval by even the better informed, who will only be interested when their own welfare is threatened. The spread of education will, there can be little doubt, tend somewhat to remedy the evils here touched on; but until the men see, by the light of a clearer understanding, that their own vice assuredly brings in its train the rupture of all household ties, and the women learn that they have rights of their own, and cannot be sold like beasts, no great advance in a right direction can be made.

Betrothals take place sometimes at a very early period of life, though it not unfrequently happens that they are deferred till the principal parties are quite of an age to choose for themselves. The betrothal should be entered in the Register; but it is not always recorded, as are not the marriages.

Widows are supposed to be free agents, but they very seldom are so, and if young, are always again disposed of by their nearest male relative. Registration of widows' marriages is so far compulsory, that if a man cannot bring forward the entry of such a marriage in the Register, his suit, unless he is otherwise provided with the clearest proofs, would assuredly be dismissed.

The betrothal and marriage ceremonies are simple. A few presents are given by the bridegroom to the bride, her parents, and her brothers; a goat is killed and *loogree* is supplied, the ceremony sometimes taking place in the house of the girl's relations, and frequently in the cottage of the bridegroom. It is customary for the newly-married woman to pay her parents a visit within a few months of her becoming a wife, and if the husband is disliked, occasion is taken to prolong the stay; nor are the man's remonstrances attended to by either the bride or her parents; the former refuses to return till she pleases, and her parents or brothers are only too glad to get her services in the cultivating season, when every hand that can be secured for field labour is of value. The loose system of betrothal and marriage, and the slender regard in which the marriage state is held, is an immense evil, and as long as this laxity of principle continues, any real amendment in the morals of the people is a sheer impossibility. There are some who deprecate special laws for special classes, but how is it practicable to fairly apply the general law of India to a people so ignorant and so long sunk in immorality as are the people of Kooloo! I consider that every betrothal, if the parents or male relations of a girl are to retain their power of betrothing her, should be only legally binding in the event of such a betrothal having been contracted prior to the girl attaining the age of fourteen, and that at this ceremony certain gifts should be allotted, and an entry made compulsory in the Register. In marriages even greater formalities are advisable, and every one of the contracting parties should be required to be present at the writing of the document, and should be bound to add their mark and take copies of the entry. It not very seldom happens that the man who desires to constitute some woman his wife, gets the Registrar to write down the regular record at his instigation, and then bribes his witnesses to come into court and swear such and such a girl has been regularly married to him! It is very difficult to create proper safeguards for females in such a population, where reading and writing are almost unknown. The men are aware, but the females are not, that if any woman remains with them and bears them children, still *she* will have no title to maintenance in his lifetime. Should he turn her off when old and ugly, she will at his death be left destitute; and, I think, there should be some special provision authorizing the civil officer to grant aid in such cases to the poor creatures thus left to shift for themselves.

In Lahoul, when a father thinks his son (perhaps only twelve years of age) should have a wife, he fixes on some particular girl, and sends to her parents a bowl of *chang* or *loogree*, which, if drunk, is a favourable sign, and if refused, the father knows he must seek elsewhere. Some months afterwards he forwards another bowl of the same drink, and should this be accepted, all is supposed to be prospering toward the coming connection. When the third bowl and a rupee are sent, and these are accepted, the whole matter is settled, and the bride, always much older than her husband, is brought to the latter by her parents. Sometimes, however, after the second instalment of liquor has been accepted, the girl objects, or her parents decline, to allow the matter to proceed further; but, then, the father of the bridegroom tries to win the girl over, if not by persuasion, by force, and, failing in the former, a lot of young fellows are sent to watch the fair one as she goes unattended to the village spring, when she is pounced upon and carried off, and locked up in some secret place, where no food is given her. Meanwhile, the person who has instigated the abduction despatches a deputation to reconcile the girl's friends, and this, as a rule, is not a very difficult operation. A great deal of talking takes place, extending over two or three days; but at last peace is made, though it frequently happens that the fair *casus belli* positively objects to even seeing the husband into whose hands she has been thus delivered, and for months refuses to speak to any one in the house; but in the end, kindness and patience bring her round, and she soon forgets her troubles. In the case of the parents of both parties consenting to a marriage, and the girl also being agreeable, certain young men are told off, and at night convey the bride to the bridegroom; but there is no marriage ceremony at all among the poorer classes, though with wealthier people the wedding is converted into something of a *spectacle*. Once in the bridegroom's house, the wife is the common property of all the brothers, and the children are liked by all their putative fathers, not one of whom can claim the special paternity of any particular child. One awkward question has arisen from this system of polyandry. In the event of a wife to four or five husbands turning

Christian, the husbands of course disclaim her, and to whom is she to turn for support? Even were she willing, her new creed would not allow her to live as she did before, and support she must expect to obtain from some one. The first husband says, "Come back to me, and I will support you"; but the wife replies, "I cannot, for though I am nominally married to you, I in reality am the wife of all your brothers." Here it seems hard to compel the husband to give maintenance, and yet the wife cannot be allowed to starve. Any day a case of this sort may turn up, and it may be because there is just this difficulty about means, that the Lahoulees are shy of listening to the missionaries.

In Spiti, according to Captain Hay, the men marry at twenty to twenty-one years of age, and the women between fifteen and twenty; and a man in good circumstances keeps two or three wives. In marriages the knot is tied by a *Lama* in the open air, when prayers are read, the sacred mark is imprinted on the forehead, and when the newly-

20

married couple enter their home white silk scarfs are presented to them by the *Lama*, who then departs, with few or many gifts, as the wealth and generosity of the parties may decide.

## CHAPTER XIII.

Sooltanpore.—Malauna.—Fairs at Sooltanpore, Plach, and Nirmand.—Doongree Temple.—Nuggur Castle.—Thakoor's House at Gondla.—Shaeshorgh Monastery.—Kee Monastery.—Dhunkur Castle—Hot Springs at Manikurn, Basisht, and Khelat.

THE only collection of houses which can, properly speaking, be termed a town, is at Sooltanpore, in the Upper Beas valley.

I have not been able to ascertain when Sooltanpore was founded, but it appears to have been, if existent, an insignificant hamlet until the reign of Rajah Juggut Sing, when it was within the territory of the Lugwuttee rajah, whose brother, Sooltan Chund, was the governor of the village, to which he apparently gave his own name. Juggut Sing, who ruled in Kooloo during the latter period of the Emperor Shah Jehan and the earlier years of Aurungzib, seized the whole of the country up the Surburri valley towards the Bubboo Pass; and Sooltan Chund being killed when defending Sooltanpore, the Rajahs of Kooloo henceforward made the place their capital, and chiefly resided their ever after. Sooltanpore is 4,092 feet above sea-level, and lies on the right bank of the Beas; it was once a regularly walled town, and, situated as it is on a natural eminence, must have been a place of some strength; but the fortifications have all been razed, and there now only remain the two gateways to the north and south, both of which are difficult of access. The palace is a large rambling building, in the style in vogue in Kooloo, with sloping slate roofs and cut-stone walls; and that and the Hindoo temple close by are the only structures within the walls worth referring to. Moorcroft passed through Sooltanpore in 1820,—it was then but an insignificant village; and Cunningham, who travelled *viâ* Kooloo to Ladakh in 1846, mentions that at that time there were only 200 of the houses inhabited, though he had learnt that in 1839 some 400 houses were in use. There are now nearly 500 houses in all, with a population that varies according to the season from 700 or 800 in summer to near 2,000 souls in autumn and spring.

To the north of the town, and just without the walls, is the *Akarah* settlement (*Akarah* meaning the resting-place of Faqueers), and several bodies of devotees are there located; but a number of shops have lately been built; these, as are all the others in the main town, being owned either by Kangra tradespeople or Lahoulees and Ladakhees. On the banks of the river, and close to the *Akarah*, is a large serai, only erected at the end of 1869, which, during the winter and spring, is filled with traders from the north. Sooltanpore is provided with a dispensary and post-office; the Tehseel, which consists of a fort-like square (in which is comprised the police-office), with an open courtyard, being to the south of the town, on an open plain; and attached to this is a small garden. The rest-house, a fairly comfortable one, lies a few hundred yards to the east of the Tehseel.

At the last census, in 1868, there were in Sooltanpore 422 houses and 1,100 inhabitants; but I am inclined to think that these figures are considerably underestimated. A large fair, partly religious and partly mercantile, takes place every year about October, in the plain to the back of the Tehseel.

The sudden increase of the Central Asian trade has tended to make Sooltanpore a place of some importance; and receiving, as it does, the entire traffic passing upwards from Kangra, the hill states, and the adjoining districts, which all stops here on its way to Leh, besides the merchandise from Eastern Turkestan and Ladakh on its downward route to Mundee and the Punjab, it is not to be wondered at that the through trade, which in 1862 was computed at £23,000, has now risen to £150,000. If this Central Asian commerce continues to prosper as it has done for the last two or three years, there is every probability of Sooltanpore becoming in time a town of considerable wealth and note.

The village of Malauna is situated on the right bank of the Malauna torrent, that joins the river Parbuttee at Jhirree. It is perhaps one of the greatest curiosities in Kooloo, as the inhabitants keep entirely to themselves, neither eating nor intermarrying with the people of any other village, and speak a language which no one but they themselves can comprehend. I subjoin a short vocabulary of some of their words, which will be found in the Appendix: this has been obligingly compiled for me by Pundit Nathoo Ram, late chief Mohurrir of Kooloo, to whom my heartiest acknowledgments are due for the aid he has given me in making researches into old records of the country. The Malauna people neither know when their village was first inhabited, nor where they themselves came from; a vague legend current in the valley ascribes the formation of the village to the hero or god

Jaemlu, *alias* Jumduggun; but this is quite a mythical individual, although temples to his honour are very numerous in Kooloo. Malauna is divided into two portions,—the upper and lower villages; the latter, built round a large square, is deemed sacred, no one being allowed to enter therein with leather shoes on. The people are all densely ignorant, no one in the place being able to read or write. The physiognomy of the inhabitants is also not a little peculiar; the eyes have a startled and frightened look, and the nose projects over the vacillating mouth, which, with the narrow chin, gives a character of feebleness to the entire face. The men dress much as do the peasantry in Kooloo, and the women wear the round brown cap, and plaids of a sober grey; but here, as in other villages, is to be seen the curious monk-like cowl of madder-brown cloth, that is carelessly adjusted across the head-piece, and allowed to hang down the shoulders.

I am inclined to believe that the Malauna villagers are a colony driven up from the plains centuries ago; they certainly have several words in use which are of Thibetan origin; but I cannot believe that their ancestors ever crossed over from the mountains in their rear, for these people have no affinity with the Bhot race; and again, the ranges that lie behind the township are quite impassable. I visited Malauna in May of this year (1870), and endeavoured then to find out all I could about this strange people, who thus hold themselves aloof from every one; but it was only subsequently that I learnt their priests have in one of the temples a gold image, which there can be very little doubt was presented to them by the Emperor Akber, who, as narrated by Abu Fuzl, visited Bajour, *i.e.* Bajoura, and Malauna. At any rate, the villagers positively assert that the great emperor did give them this token of his regard; but whether it was, as they say, a likeness of himself, an image, or merely a gold coin with his effigy on it, I am not now able to find out.

It was for long the custom in Malauna to

settle all disputes before a local tribunal. The priests at specified times called all the villagers up, absentees being fined for non-attendance. The assembly being gathered together, the priests demanded who had complaints to bring forward, and when a case was deemed deserving of consideration, and there were doubts as to the way in which judgment should go, each claimant brought out a goat, and at the same moment cutting open the thigh and inserting poison in the wound, victory was pronounced to fall to him whose goat first died!

The principal fairs in Kooloo are at Sooltanpore, in October; at Plach (Bunjar), in May; and at Nirmand at variable dates in the autumn. The Sooltanpore fair takes place at the Dusseerah festival, and a considerable amount of business is transacted, though the meeting is more of a religious than of a mercantile character. At this festival the people lay in their stock of shoes, brass and copper pots, and such-like articles, which are not made up in Kooloo, and the women renew their coloured wools for the hair, and their jewellery, and pretty head-dresses. The *mela*, which used to be, and probably now is, the most celebrated in the valley, was in old days an event of no little interest to the people, as it was customary to bring some 360 local deities to pay their respects to the presiding shrine of Rugonath Ji; but of late the attendance has fallen off, and not more than seventy or eighty of the minor divinities are now brought up; on this occasion, however, the followers of each particular idol do their best to show to advantage, and every banner, trumpet, and drum that are available are put into requisition. The fair goes on for nearly a week; and for several days before it commences, all the roads leading to Sooltanpore are thronged with gaily-dressed crowds of men, women, and children, bearing in procession the god of their own hamlet; on arrival at the plain near the town, encampments are formed, and shortly after the various adherents of particular shrines begin marching about, and parade all their magnificence as a sort of preliminary spectacle and foretaste of what will be done on the opening and the final days of the entertainment. The devotees attached to the Rugonath shrine have not in the meanwhile been idle, and by the morning, when the fair really commences, the *rath* or wooden temple, which lies in the plain all the year round, has been provided with wheels, and liberally ornamented with coloured cloths and flowers, and all being ready for the reception of the idol, this is placed on a species of seat inside the framework. All local deities are now brought up, with such *addenda* of pomp and music as are procurable, and are arranged round the central figure. The high priest then steps out in front, and with every appearance of extreme devotion, prays to the god, and sprinkles water before the shrine; and the leading men of Kooloo, headed by the representative of the old sovereigns of the country, now walk rapidly three times round the *rath*, amid the incessant bray of the trumpets, and beating of cymbals and tomtoms. Stout ropes are next attached to the lower timbers of the *rath*, which is borne along for a few hundred yards by an enthusiastic crowd, followed by all the smaller gods, and again is brought back to its place, when the people separate and repair to their own camps, or swarm round the shops spread over the plain. On the closing day the same ceremonies are enacted; and now the car is carried almost right into the river Beas, and a sheep or goat being killed, and a clay figure of Lanka, the enemy of Rugonath, being decapitated, the latter is supposed to have obtained the victory over his foes, and is drawn back again to the plain, is then taken once more to his temple, and shortly after the fair breaks up.

The Plach fair, in May, is equally well attended as is the one at Sooltanpore, and forms the central place of gathering to the Seoraj *kothees*. A good deal of real business is done at this *mela*, principally in sheep and goats, which are bought up by butchers for the Simla market at from four shillings to five shillings apiece.

The great fair at Nirmand, nearly opposite Rampore, in Bussahir, comes off every twelve years. The legend concerning Nirmand, although clouded in ridiculous fable, is not altogether unworthy of note. The great Purus Ram, having, by his father's desire, killed his mother Ranka, procured her restoration to life after performing various acts of filial obedience; but being regarded with universal detestation for slaying her who had given him birth, he expiated his offence by giving lands to Brahmins; among which were five villages on the Sutledj, by name Kao, Mael, Nuggur, Nirt, and Nirmand. At the latter place he presented the Brahmins with a goddess, named Ambka, and as he regarded her as his special divinity, he instructed the priests to hold a *yug*, or feast, in her honour every three years, and it has therefore been an immemorial custom in Nirmand to celebrate this festival. At an interval of every twelve years, is the most celebrated *yug*, called

*Boonda;* three years after comes *Boondajee;* three after that, *Butpoor,* and three again afterwards, *Sandh.* The statue of Purus Ram is only shown every twelfth year, and for the three years before it is exhibited spices are perpetually burnt, in honour of Ambka, near Purus Ram's temple. Six months before the twelfth yearly festival a *Bedar* begins the preparation of the rope by which he is to be swung over the cliff; and every day this man washes and works, and is only assisted by one individual, no other person being permitted to come near or speak to him. The cable being pronounced ready, the local deities of Kao, Mael, Nirt, and Nuggur* are summoned to Nirmand, their priests being paid for attending, and if they cannot be induced to bring their gods, no fair can be held. Supposing everything is in order, Purus Ram's temple is opened, and two or three of the priests with closed eyes

* This Nuggur must not be confused with the Nuggur in the Upper Beas valley.

go inside and take out the idol, and whatever else they may inadvertently touch. In the last *Boonda*, which took place in 1868, the following articles were produced: an axe of Purus Ram's, weighing forty pounds; a *guggur*, or pot of brass; a bow and arrow; some iron bullets, and a large shell. In the hand of the statue is a copper sheet, on which the priests affirm are the title-deeds of their jagheer, as written by the donor!

The statue is then put in the upper storey of the temple, and the belief is that it perspires every day. However this may be, what answers for perspiration is mixed with water and distributed among the people, who receive it with reverence. Each day that the idol stays outside, forty pounds of spices are burnt, and on the great day of the fair the statue is taken to the *Akarah*, and allowed to remain there one hour, while all worship. A procession then winds round the temple, and every ten or twelve paces a goat, then a sheep, and then a pig are killed. Just before Purus Ram's image is put into the *Akarah*, the *Bedar* and his companion take the rope they have been preparing to the spot previously arranged upon, and there fix one end firmly into the cliff, and the idol, being now in the *Akarah*, the *Bedar* is slung to the rope, which is sloped off to the ground some distance below. A running wheel is secured round the rope to aid in the gliding of the *Bedar*, and bags of earth are fastened to the legs of the martyr ostensibly to break his fall. During the *Boonda* of 1856 this wheel stuck in the cable, and to aid the *Bedar's* descent, the people tautened the rope till it broke; the *Bedar* was killed; but it is said that no accident had ever occurred before. Colonel Lake, then Commissioner of the division, hearing of this accident, forbade the repetition of the dangerous sport, and at the last fair a goat was substituted for a human victim. Directly the *Bedar* touched the ground, Purus Ram's statue was taken again into the temple, with everything that had been brought out of the building. The priests assert that there is an enormous snake in the temple, so that they dare not go in with their eyes open! When the idol is placed within, the following articles are also deposited in the edifice: twelve years' supply of toothbrushes (one for each day), a *guggur* or brass pot, full of water, from a well that is immediately closed and not opened till the ensuing *Boonda*, and a lighted *chiragh* or oil lamp, which, it is declared, never goes out. The Nirmand temples are very old, but they have been constantly repaired; and within the last few years local subscriptions were got up, and the Ambka temple was entirely reroofed with copper sheets. Some of the Nirmand Brahmins have come from Cashmere, and others from Kashi, or Benares, *i.e.* Bernashi, separation of castes.

It will be as well, in speaking of the more noted buildings in the subdivision, to select only such as present some peculiarly interesting features. Of the temples, perhaps the one that, of all others, deserves notice here, is the one at Doongree, about half a mile to the west of the encamping-ground at Menalee. This temple is a very large and peculiarly-made one, and is twenty-eight feet in breadth by forty-six feet in length. On three sides there is a verandah, and the doorway, which is to the east, is covered with rude carvings in wood of elephants, birds, tigers, and Buddhistical wheels; the story being that the then reigning sovereign of Kooloo, to prevent the artist ever making a duplicate of such a masterpiece, cut off the carver's right hand. But, not to be baffled, the man taught his left hand to take the place of the lost member, and at Triloknath, in Chumba, executed an even finer piece of carving than that at Doongree. Here again, however, adverse fortune followed him, for the Triloknath people, determined that no such workmanship should be ever exhibited elsewhere, now cut off his head! The Doongree temple is of most massive construction, but is clumsily put together, and is quite out of the perpendicular. The verandahs are twelve feet above the ground, and the roof, formed of huge deodar planks, slopes over these. Then comes a superstructure which bears up another sloping roof, on the top of which is again some fancy woodwork, that is surmounted by another roof with the same incline as have those below, all being of a shape to fit the four-square lie of the temple; but on the top is fixed a circular umbrella-like cone of deodar planks, which has fallen considerably to the north side, being ornamented on the summit by a brass ball and trident. The interior of the temple can only be seen from the doorway, and none but those of the highest castes can go inside. The goddess Hurimba, to whom the building is dedicated, and who is said to have lived in Purus Ram's time, is represented by a small brass image three inches in height, contrasting most ludicrously in point of size with the temple, that stands a good eighty feet above the ground. The construction of this edifice is much ruder than what is usually met with in Kooloo, and notably most inferior to the temple in the same style at Dhyar, opposite Bajoura; but the structure is held in great veneration, and, situated as it is in the deep gloom of an extensive pine forest, it becomes a very striking object. In the interior there are large rocks, and a rope hangs from the roof, to which legends have it human victims were, in old times, suspended by the hands after death, and swung to and fro over the goddess. On the northern portal of the entrance is the effigy of a snake in iron. Close by are two picturesque and ruined houses, which were once the *dhurmsalas*, or resting-places for devotees; they are both fast falling to pieces, and are mainly used by the woodcutters in the forest. The date of erection of the Doongree temple is uncertain; but, though the present building is of no great age, it is highly probable that it stands in the place, and is the facsimile of a structure coeval with the earliest days of Kooloo.

Nuggur Castle, the old place of residence of the Kooloo sovereigns, is situated on a rising knoll on the left shore of the Beas, than which river it is about a thousand feet higher. Off the main building, which, there can be little doubt, once contained the principal apartments of the rajahs and their establishments, stretch a range of kitchens and out-offices, the separate approach to which is by a long flight of steps, that from below are lost to sight in the deep gloom of the passage, and at the back stands a square serai of two storeys, with an open interior courtyard. The castle has a northerly aspect, and commands a fine view of the Lahoul and Rohtung peaks, and from the west it overlooks the valley, which spreads below, intersected by the Beas, that meanders with many a picturesque bend, and is for the most part lost to sight behind the thick woodland that hems in its banks. Rising on the other side are the Bara Banghal peaks, which here tower to a height of about 13,000 feet. The entrance (on the north) is by a small flight of stairs that lead to a verandah of comparatively recent construction, which, however, only extends itself in front of the central apartments. In the lower storey the rooms to the east and centre are merely used for lumber, but the apartment to the west has been fitted up for European residence, and is both commodious and airy, its height being about twenty-two feet. Wooden stairs lead to the upper verandah, from which there is a very beautiful and extensive prospect. From this verandah one enters the drawing and dining-room, the corresponding door on the other side conducting to a covered and glass-windowed verandah, which runs the whole length of the back. The room to the west is similar in form to the one below, and has, as has the latter, two deeply embayed windows, and the only fireplace the structure boasts of. The east room has, till lately, been used as a tea-store, and from it a rude verandah leads to the kitchens, which lie south-east of the front of the house, and are, with their projecting eaves and fanciful carved woodwork, by far the most picturesque part of the castle. Behind the Anglicised portion of the building is an open courtyard flush with the floor of the verandah, and behind this again is the serai, now used as a stable and for servants' quarters.

Nuggur Castle, occupying, as it does, such a commanding site, cannot fail, from its great size, to attract the notice of the passer-by even at some distance off, for the windows of the upper storey are certainly nearly forty feet above the foundations, and below these the ground slopes rapidly away at a very steep incline for several hundred feet. A certain chief of Kooloo, Rajendra Pal, is said to have first made Nuggur his residence, but it is doubtful whether the present town can claim to be even the remains of the former capital; for the popular belief is that a large extent of ruin, termed Thawa, some little distance up the hill-side, to the east of the castle, was the actual city of old times. For some sixty successive reigns Nuggur or Thawa appears to have been honoured with the presence of the ruling chiefs. In the reign of Rajah Juggut Sing, about A.D. 1650, it is stated that the present Nuggur Castle was erected out of the ruins of Thawa, but the capital was removed to Sooltanpore at this period; and, by the time the country was given over to the British by the Sikhs, the building was in a most ruinous state. It was taken up by Captain Hay, the first Assistant-Commissioner of Kooloo, as his head-quarters, and he put it into repair, and sold the estate when he retired from the service; it has lately, however, been bought in by the Punjab Government for the official residence of the Assistant-Commissioner in charge of the subdivision.

The *Thakoor's* house at Gondla, in Lahoul, is one that is well worthy of some brief notice, as it is the largest structure in Lahoul, and quite unique in its formation. It is of no mean dimensions, and very strongly built of timber and stones, cemented together with wet clay, as indeed are all the Lahoul houses. Within the building are many rooms, some very large, and one of these, supported by many uprights, would certainly comfortably accommodate 100 persons; there are others also, with open verandahs, that are hardly much smaller. The peculiar feature about this house is the high tower, which contains six or seven storeys, the staircase from one room to the other being constructed of notched logs. In one apartment is shown a cooking-place that was used by the Kooloo rajah Maun Sing (cir. A.D. 1720) when proceeding on pilgrimage to Triloknath; and, on a beam in the roof is to be seen an order of this chief, in the Nagari character; but it is so defaced by age and smoke that it is now quite illegible. At the very top of the house are hung all the winter supplies of warm clothing, but the most interesting of all the chambers are the two devoted to the worship of Buddha; in the outer one of which, that was, at the time of my visit, most scrupulously clean, were pictures suspended on the walls, and a couple of flat drums pendent from the ceiling, and furnished with carved legs, that rested on the ground. In the inner apartment or oratory, which also was very neat and clean, and smelt most strongly of incense, were the array of family gods, that were concealed in a recess in the wall, at the back of a shutter-screen, which the *Thakoor* removed. This screen was painted all over somewhat tastefully, and behind it were the idols, some of which had been brought all the way from Shagatze and Lhassa. I was also shown an open cabinet, resembling in size and form an open back-gammon board, filled with what appeared to be terra cotta impressions of figures, really most excellently and artistically finished;* these, however, are not of native manufacture,—they come from Lhassa, as do most of the objects used in Buddhist worship, though I believe many of the bells and brass implements are imported *viâ* Ladakh from Nepal. In 1869 such heavy rain set in while I was at Gondla, that I was only too glad to accept the *Thakoor's*

* Since the above was written, I have managed to secure this work of art at a cost of £3, and I shall hope shortly to place it in some museum in England.

offer of a room in this house; and although my cell-like apartment was provided with only a door, for it was all open in front, it secured me a shelter from the inclemencies of the weather, and afforded an excellent opportunity of rambling at will over the strange mansion, and of observing, in my detention of two or three days, all the internal household arrangements of one of the largest landholders in Lahoul.

The largest monasteries in the subdivision are in Spiti, but the Shaeshorgh one in Lahoul is not altogether undeserving of a separate description. This lamasery lies on the hill behind Kielung, and is approached by a steep but not difficult path, and some very fine views are to be had in its vicinity of the snowy ranges and the enormous glacial beds that stretch between them. The building, a rectangular block, plastered over with mud and whitewashed, has a flat roof, ornamented with little flags, rude but strong verandahs projecting from the walls; some tumble-down old houses are quite close by, and in these the *Lamas* live, of whom when I visited the place in August, 1868, there were but two in residence. Opposite the entrance-gate of the monastery, there is, across what might be either termed a gallery or lobby, another door, which leads into a lofty apartment used as the kitchen; but turning to the left, and following the line of the dark corridor, and passing a large collection of prayer-wheels, an open court to the right is approached, equal in area to the kitchen; and looking through a doorway in this, one can see through the intense gloom a low room, lit up by a small skylight. The roof of this chamber is supported by massive beams, which were garnished with belts, swords, yaks' tails, huge and horrible masks, feathers, and all sorts of odds and ends; between the pillars were strings, on which necklaces of dried flowers of a most delicious odour were arranged; and on the left were the huge flat drums, fixed into a stand and supported on staves. Curious feather-like crosses hung from every nook and corner, and to these were fastened scraps of what seemed to be leaves of some wild plant, which floated about in the air, and relieved with their colour the sombre darkness around. Quaint and fantastic masks, covered with cloths and tricked with black chowries,* were intermingled with the curious drum-sticks, vessels of all sorts, and the numberless other objects, which in the gloom could not be identified. Round the walls were paintings in brilliant colours; and in one corner was a large painted revolving prayer-wheel, full of prayers, the ends of its axes being in the ceiling and floor; the devotee turns this round, a bell being struck after one complete revolution, when all the prayers inside the vat are supposed to have been uttered,—a most comfortable and convenient religion for those who can't find time to pray for themselves or some one to pray for them. The main objects of interest in this "chamber of horrors" are the figures of Buddha, and other attendant divinities, which are arranged

* Yaks' tails.

somewhat like actors on a stage, or, more properly speaking, like figures in a waxwork show; the gloom of the place being rather deepened by the green curtain that hangs from the roof just within the skylight. Along the raised recess sunk into the wall sit the draped and ghostly figures of the gods; Buddha himself, of giant size and dwarfing all the others, is coloured a pale white, and round him is loosely thrown a flowing robe of purple and white calico. The remaining images are likewise swathed in clothes, but the feeble light from above but partially falls upon the ghastly array, and it is with difficulty that the features or contours can be traced. In front stretches a wooden trestle, with seven censers of brass; and in the middle of the floor is a block of timber, on which stands another censer full of oil, containing a wick, that is lighted to show the interior to visitors. The perpendicular face of the idol platform is painted in arabesques in vermilion, blue, and white.

The Kee monastery is the largest in Spiti, and is situated between Khiebur and Kazeh, just over the small village of Kee, on the left bank of the Spiti river. As seen from the Khiebur side, it presents the appearance of a hill fort crowning an eminence, a vast wall of rock rising over it to the east, and thus affording some shelter from the prevailing winds. In August, 1869, I went over this *lamasery*, and examined with much interest the chapels, storehouses, and dormitories of the monks; but in summer very few of the *Lamas* are in residence, the majority living in their own villages till the winter snows once more recall them within the sacred walls. Some 200 or 300 monks are in this monastery in the winter, the cells, over eighty in number, being then all filled. There are many apartments for the priests, and the storehouses are filled to overflowing with supplies for the winter, and with the dresses, musical instruments, masks, and other necessities for occasions of religious ceremony. In the refectory at the time of my visit I had an opportunity of seeing the monks prepare their food, which was simmering in large caldrons over a blazing fire, while one of the neophytes churned the tea in a long wooden barrel, bound round with several brass rings. The passages from one chamber to the other are in absolute darkness, and to enable one to see the way over the worn-out and unequal steps, torches have to be lighted. The great chapel was very much in the same style as the one at Shaëshorgh, in Lahoul, but, of course, much larger and much better fitted up; and here there was a screen of brightly coloured silks, behind which were the deities, ranged in about the same order as in other *lamaseries*. Egerton, in page 22 of his "Tour in Spiti," quotes from Cosmo de Koros, who states that "in the eleventh century, in the time of Atisha, a learned man of Bengal, Buddhism, that had been nearly abolished in the tenth century, commenced again to revive in Thibet. This celebrated pundit (Atisha), upon repeated invitations, at last visited that snowy country, going first to Guge, in Nari (Nari Khorsum), and afterwards to Utsang (Lhassa), where he remained till his death in

1052. Bromston, or Brom, his pupil, founded the Rugring monastery (still existing), and with him originated the Kadampa sect, from which afterwards issued that of Gelupka." As Egerton points out, Rareng, or, as it is sometimes called, Rangrig, is a large village across the Spiti river, nearly opposite the Kee monastery, and there can be little doubt that the *lamasery* founded by Bromston is the identical one at Kee, the date of its erection being somewhere about A.D. 1000.

Dhunkur Castle, in Spiti, is in reality but a number of houses collected together on the crest of a huge clayey promontory that overhangs the left bank of the Spiti river. There may, perhaps, have once been a fort here; but if so, no traces of such a work are now visible, and no appliances of a defensive nature are to be found anywhere near. One large room is not unseldom used by passing travellers; and in August, 1869, I put up in this for a short time. From it, corridors cut in the rock pass to other chambers, which are either used as store-rooms for grass, fuel, corn, or any lumber the villagers please. Below, descend in tiers the houses of the town, which is of some size, and on another promontory, a little further on, is the Dhunkur monastery, that abounds in dark passages and breakneck staircases, with some very ugly falls down the cliff, if a false step be taken. Dhunkur is certainly a curious old place, and well worthy of a visit. I believe it was once the residence of the governor of the valley, when Spiti was held by Ladakh.

In Kooloo there are hot springs at Manikurn, Basisht, and Khelat, the two former being of considerable note.

The village of Manikurn lies toward the head of the Parbuttee valley, on the right bank of the Parbuttee river, and consists of some seven or eight Hindoo temples and fifty or sixty houses; one of the temples being much of the same form as the ones at Byjnath in Kangra, and at Bajoura and other places in the Upper Beas valley. To this particular structure is joined on a low rectangular block roofed with slabs of slate, and the foundations of the edifice stand some feet below the level of the ground. The people of the place say that this sinking occurred some hundreds of years ago, when the Parbuttee flooded the town, and they point to the cracks in the walls, and the curious lie of the joists and beams, which are quite out of the horizontal or perpendicular, in corroboration of this theory; but it has been doubted on good authority whether any sudden sinking of the soil on which the buildings rest ever took place, and the differences of level are attributed to artificial causes, and the irregularities in the woodwork to the effect of an earthquake. This temple at Manikurn is in honour of Mahadeo, the others being dedicated to minor deities. The particular specialty of Manikurn are the hot springs, which have long been noted places of resort for devotees, who come to this shrine even from Madras! The jet that used to be the most important has within the last few years been gradually dying out, the ground all round being curiously marked, as if by the action of fire and water, streaks of vivid chrome and burnt sienna alternating with what appear to be formations of a decidedly volcanic nature. The second spring, down by the river's bank, is still in full play, but its waters can hardly be utilized. The third spring, however, bubbles up by several jets in a species of natural basin in the rocky soil, and may be twelve feet in circumference by a foot and a half deep.

This spring is always in great activity, and is said to rise and fall with the Parbuttee, being in temperature above boiling point, so that the rice which it is *de rigueur* for all pilgrims to have cooked in the pool, is prepared for consumption without further trouble to the owner than placing the grain in a bag, tying this at the mouth with a string, and throwing the same into the water. All round the rocks are too hot to bear the touch of the naked hand, and the air is impregnated with a distinct odour of sulphur;

but the water is not unpleasant to the taste; and the rice cooked in it is just as palatable as if prepared in the usual manner. There are several covered tanks for bathing purposes, and the waters are said to be found of benefit in rheumatism and skin diseases.

The little village of Basisht is situated on the left bank of the Beas, about two miles to the north of the Menalee encampment. It boasts of one of the pyramidal stone temples, erected, it is said, in the reign of Rajah Juggut Sing, about 1650, and is much like the one at Bajoura in size and adornments, but, as a work of art, very much the inferior of the latter. Hoonyman is here the presiding deity. This temple has its gateway to the west (while the entrance to the Bajoura one is to the east), and is covered with a rectangular wooden framework, supported by slanting poles, which are let into the main structure. There are three hot springs at Basisht, but the two upper ones have very little water, the lower one being the most active and the most celebrated. It gushes out of the ground into a small tank, which leads again into a regular bath, one channel for the superfluous fluid leading by the high encircling walls, and finding an exit, as does the surplus water of the bath, into a lower open apartment that is used for ablutionary purposes by the inferior castes. Each of these baths is about twenty feet square, and the upper one is provided with steps for the convenience of bathers, and has a flat pediment of stone, arranged all round for the use of visitors. Two inscriptions, in a character I cannot decipher, have been cut in the walls, and copies of these I attach in the Appendix. Adjoining the spring is a rectangular stone and wood temple, dedicated to Ram Chundur and also to Vashishta Muni, after whom this village, by a change of the *V* into *B* and striking off the final *a*, takes its name. Undoubtedly this temple is far more ancient than the pyramidal one before noticed. The temperature of the hot spring is very nearly at boiling point; but I have had no means of testing the heat. Where the water first issues, the hand cannot be held in the basin; and if the bath be rapidly filled, it becomes impossible to use it for several hours after. Cunningham, in page 11 of his "Journal of a Trip through Kooloo," thus explains the tradition with regard to the saint Vashishta Muni, "to whom common tradition assigns the origin of the name of the Beas," and who, being weary of life, tied his hands and feet together and threw himself into the river, which burst his bonds and floated him safe on shore. Just above Menalee and the place where Basisht now stands, "the valley of the Beas closes in, and the gneiss rocks which have been thrust up through the mica-slate are scarped on both sides of the valley, forming opposing cliffs, which rise to a height somewhat greater than the level of Menalee and Vashishta Muni." Cunningham goes on to state that the spur on the left bank of the Beas probably "once extended right across the valley and pent up the river, which must then have formed a large lake, the bottom of which was the extensive alluvial flat of Menalee, which could only have been formed in this manner. Indeed, there is every appearance of a lake in this part of the bed of the Beas, from which the waters made their escape between the gneiss cliffs, just below Menalee and Vashishta Muni. When the lake existed, the hot spring must have been covered by its waters. In the course of time, as the gneiss rocks were either gradually worn down, or suddenly rent asunder and swept away by the Beas river, the hot springs of Vashishta Muni were brought to light, or, to use the language of the legends, the bonds of Vashishta Muni were burst by the waters of the river, which was afterwards called Vipasa,* or the boundless." The above is a very ingenious piece of reasoning, and if not true, deserves to be so.

Khelat is an insignificant hamlet of three or four houses, on the right bank of the Beas,

* The Beas in Sanskrit is called the Vipasa.

some twenty miles to the north of Sooltanpore. There is one hot spring here, which is of a bitter taste, and whose waters, standing at a temperature of 104° Fahr., are received in an open tank about twelve feet square and three deep. This spring is in no repute.

## CHAPTER XIV.

**Carvings at Bajoura Temple.—Sculptured Stones at Nuggur.—Sculptures at Juggutsookh.—Carvings at Shumshee.**

THE best sculptured remains in Kooloo are to be seen in the pyramidal stone temple near Bajoura, ten miles below Sooltanpore. To enter into a full account of the various carvings in this temple would take up too much space, but it may not be amiss to dwell briefly on some of the leading features of these works of an unknown artist. To outward appearance, it seems there is a good deal of similarity between the form of part of the Byjnath temple and this one; but the former has a porch, which the Bajoura one is not supplied with, and is also literally covered with carvings, whereas the temple under notice has not many sculptures, though all it possesses are good of their kind. This structure is in the form of an elongated beehive, with a great deal of carved stone-work, and three recesses containing figures on the north, south, and west fronts, the doorway being to the east. The interior, perhaps twelve or fourteen feet square, has been built up of large layers of stone well cut, but not cemented with plaster; and an earthquake, or some falling away of the subsoil, has thrown the great mass of the masonry to the south side, and without actually disengaging the blocks, has torn them from their original positions, leaving great gaps in the wall; the side stones, the uprights of which form the massive doorway, have also been twisted half round, and on the south side part of the superstructure actually overhangs. There is no arch in the building, the roof being made up of layers of stone lapping over each other, as in the Hindoo buildings at the colonnade in the Kootub at Delhi. The height of the entrance was, as nearly as I could estimate, about six feet four inches. The whole of the exterior is richly carved, and the summit is crowned with what might be termed an enormous circular stone with ribbed radiating protuberances, presenting something of the appearance of a compressed melon or pumpkin. Over each front is an oval hollow, containing one full face and a half-face on either flank; the faces in the oval to the west side having a most Grecian aspect, and not being at all in the Hindoo style of art, the eyes of the central figure being large and full, and the other features in good keeping. On the southern side of the temple there is a figure of a god a good deal mutilated. This is Gunaesh, with an elephant's head, the right hand holding a battleaxe, the pose of the hand being very good: the left hand also grasps some article that is too much injured for recognition. Apparently there were two other arms, but only fragments of what might have been these limbs now remain. A string passes from the left shoulder and winds round the stomach, being then again brought to the right side; the right leg is tucked up, the heel being under the stomach, and the left leg in the usual sitting posture. Both these limbs are much damaged (as is the head), and they are not equal in execution to the arms. The figure rests on what might be leaves, and below on either side are mutilated lions having their paws crossed in front, and in the interior space between the lions there is a small human figure, but so broken up that nothing can be made of it. The pose of Gunaesh's image is good and even majestic.

In the doorway (to the east) the portals on either flank are adorned with carved figures, the subject on the right (as one enters) representing a female, crowned in very much the same way that Porus, the Indian king, is supposed to have been, three tiers of necklets terminating in a pendant between the breasts, which, with the face, have been broken off; the right arm hangs down to the elbow, the hand being raised to a level with the head, and holding a species of vase, which might contain either flowers or incense. The left arm, ornamented, like the right, with armlets, leans a little from the side, but the hand rests on the thigh, or rather below it, and holds a wreath of flowers, which stretch up in a flowing pattern above. The figure bends to its left side, but the frame is equally poised on both legs, the left leg being rather advanced. A species of trouser, rather tight, and marked with transverse bands, comes up to the middle, and below this, and running across the middle, is a broad girdle, from which hang ornaments of a bell shape. The feet are bare, but have very large anklets, that cross the front of the instep. To the figure's left side is a smaller statuette, very much injured; a woman, leaning, as it were, on the bank to the right, shows the whole of the right leg, the left one, below the knee, being drawn to the rear; the right hand, which is well carved, holds a pole that runs down to the feet, the left arm being in repose.

The opposite subject is in good preservation, but the woman's face and part of the breasts and left arm are broken. The pose is much the same as in the one just described, the left arm also holding a vase; but the right leg is here advanced, instead of the left, and the right arm is extended, and appears, while it grasps a stalk of some flowering shrub, to rest on the head of a kneeling and smaller figure, which is almost destroyed. Behind this last there is another form, apparently of a female. The pose of the larger figure is really good. Each of the entablatures in the entrance is about two feet in height.

The sculpturing on the north face of the temple is the best preserved of all. A halo, ornamented on the outer border with what I take to be acanthus leaves, spreads round the upper part of the statue of Ashtbhoorjee; the head, a good deal injured, is crowned and ornamented with earrings. The body and limbs are out of proportion, and yet they evince some knowledge of anatomy in the sculptor, and the proportions in parts are good, but the length of the trunk and arms is excessive. The neck has three necklets, terminating in a pendant; the breasts have been broken off, and round the stomach is a cincture of an angular shape; while trousers, as in the figures in the entrance, cover the legs to the feet. There are eight arms. On the right side there is one grasping a trident (much injured), a second holds something I could not decipher, a third has a species of dart, and a fourth clasps a sword. The arms on the left come as follows:—The foremost seizes the hair of a crouching figure, into the body of which the trident is being plunged; the second holds a bell,—and here the carving and pose are exceedingly good; a third holds a censer, and the fourth a bow. The right leg is lifted up, and the foot rests on the leg of the recumbent figure, whose right hand is endeavouring to release Ashtbhoorjee's grasp in its hair, while its left arm is encircled by an oblong shield. Ashtbhoorjee's left leg is planted on the ground to its left side. Just below the end of the bow is a small figure, with the right arm upraised over the head. The crouching man under Ashtbhoorjee has his legs wide apart, and apparently rests on some animal, which is mutilated past all identification.

On the western face of the temple, in a recess similar to those on the northern and southern sides, is the statue of a man with a triple crown and a halo, on the upper ends of which are two bosses of figures.* The hands here are well portrayed, but the body is badly put together, and the legs are very indifferently executed. Coins or feathers cover the top of the head and flow down behind, and heavy earrings are

* It is somewhat curious that there is a facsimile of this piece of sculpturing near Byjnath temple, in Kangra; but the latter is of very inferior execution, and has, in addition to the figures found in the Bajoura carving, the statue of a woman of the same size as the man. This, probably, also existed in the Bajoura specimen, but was broken off, so as to allow the remainder of the entablature to be inserted in the limited space which the Bajoura temple afforded.

worn, with several necklets; these last not being furnished with pendants. There are four arms. The two on the right hold what might be flowers; one on the left is broken off, and the other grasps a sword, very like the sort of singlestick used in native games: the pose of the sword hand is excellent. From the left shoulder to the right side passes the holy thread; short trousers cover the limbs to above the knee, and an ornamental girdle, in a species of coil, descends from the left shoulder, falls below the knee, and ascends up the other flank. On the left of the statue is a woman with a triple crown, the right hand holding a censer or flowers, the left following the incline of the body and resting on the left leg, the frame being supported on the right leg. This is the only female figure in the temple the bust of which has not been injured. On the other side of the four-armed god is the form of a man, equal in size to that of the woman, and about half as large as the central figure. The male statuette is almost the counterpart of the female one, but it only has a double crown, and holds in its left hand a smaller flower, and in the right what may be either a torch or a *chowrie.*

The whole of this temple is richly carved in a floriated pattern, and I think it would be highly desirable to have a set of photographs secured of the various sculpturings, ere further damage renders them quite unrecognizable.

This temple, *as it stands now*, is certainly purely Hindoo, and the Lingam inside points it out as being dedicated to Shiva. In Shiva's shrines the softer emotions find no place, and the female figure is represented, if at all, as an object of terror or dread; but in this structure the smaller figures in the entrance would seem to set forth the gentler sex in a pleasing form, and it may be that not only these, but the three larger entablatures, were added some time after Buddhism and the worship of Shiva had disappeared from Kooloo; and there is some ground for this supposition, as the stone casts are in all cases mutilated at the corners and base, and it is not unlikely they were placed in their present position long after the temple was built; but it is pressing the argument too far, perhaps, to insist upon anything of this sort. If this is a temple built and dedicated to Shiva, as it seems to have been, I am inclined to place the date of its erection about the eleventh, or perhaps the tenth century of our era, at a time when Buddhism must have been dying away in Kooloo, and considerably prior to the promulgation of the worship of Vishnoo, which was not, it is said, in force until Rajah Juggut Sing's reign, about the year 1640 A.D.

At Nuggur there is a curious collection of what resemble tombstones, that are to be found just below Nuggur Castle. They are inserted into the ground in four rows, rising one over the other on the hill-side; and in all I have counted 141 of these, each ornamented with rude carvings of chiefs of Kooloo, their wives and concubines being portrayed either beside them or in lines below. One rajah is mounted on a horse, and holds a sword in his hand, the animal he bestrides being covered with housings, just as might be a Crusader's charger; a very similar figure to this is carved in wood over the porch of the Doongree temple. The report is that these stones were placed in position at the death of every reigning sovereign of Kooloo, the female figures being the effigies of such wives or mistresses who may have performed *suttee* at their lord's demise. If this be the true state of the case, then the human sacrifices must have been very great in some instances, for it is not uncommon to find forty and fifty female figures crowding the crumbling and worn surface of the stones. At the death of the late Rae Gyan Sing, the representative of a once powerful family, his servants executed a rude effigy of him, and this will take its place beside the other funeral relics of his ancestors. The Buddhist wheel appears in several of the stones, but the people about Nuggur positively declare that none of these rough sculpturings are over 200 years of age; here, however, I think they are mistaken, and they know so very little about the history of their own country that anything they say that refers to dates must be received with great caution. Apart from this collection is a rude statue of a woman, half imbedded in the ground, the tradition concerning which is, that one of the queens of a Kooloo rajah, being suspected of infidelity, threw herself, in a fit of indignation, out of the castle windows, and was turned into a stone image before she reached the earth, wherein she has lain ever since. As the statue is only some three feet high, we may suppose the women of Kooloo were smaller in those days than they are now.

At Juggutsookh, in the Upper Beas valley, there are some most interesting carvings, that are quite unique both in design and execution. They are kept in the rectangular temple in front of General Conynghame's bungalow, and probably belong to some ancient edifice which has long been destroyed, and the fragments of which lie piled up in confusion about the village. I took the opportunity, when at Juggutsookh, to have some of these sculpturings brought outside. One of them, a broken entablature of Kale, is rather over two feet in length. It is peculiar both because the hands and feet are well drawn, and because, in front of the figure, the hands support a large bowl. The whole work is cut out of solid stone, but unfortunately there is a breakage that somewhat damages the left side of the image. Kale is depicted with four hands: one on the right holds a torch, the other supports the bowl, and one of the left hands clutches a species of framework, which, however, may be meant for clothing, and the other aids in supporting the bowl. The upper portion of the figure is nude, and a garland or string of snakes is wound round the neck, and falls to the feet. The face is a better one than is usually met with. The headpiece is made of three peaks, and, standing out horizontally below the ears, are curious shell-like tapering ornaments. The right foot rests on a bull, but this last is much broken. The bowl, that is very like a highly-finished *ghurra* with an ornamented top, has a large hole in the centre that goes right through the body of the statue, which, in all probability, was once used as a cistern.

There are many other sculpturings in *alto relievo* in this temple, and perhaps, after the one of Kale, the next best worthy of attention is an entablature, a little over a foot in height, which represents Shiva and Parbuttee riding, or rather sitting, in a semi-recumbent attitude on a bull.* Shiva has an aureole round his head and shoulders, and holds in his right hand a trident; and Parbuttee has three snakes depicted over her head. This piece of sculpture is very much damaged, but is so far remarkable, as it is the only one

* A similar carving to this one is to be found on the north wall of the enclosure of the Byjnath temple, in Kangra; but in this last Parbuttee has only one snake near her, and this is grasped by Shiva.

out of a vast number I have seen in Kooloo which bears the effigies of snakes, and this although separate figures of snakes in both iron and wood are not at all uncommon in the temples in the Upper Beas valley. In this Juggutsookh temple there are also two Buddhistical circles in the roof, exactly the same as those depicted in the photographs of the Tope at Amravati. Outside the porch are two sitting lions, and the remains of various small Lingams are scattered about the rude courtyard in front. The mixture of relics of Buddhism and Hindoo worship is not a little curious.

Not a hundred yards below Shumshee, which is perhaps five miles to the north of Bajoura, on the road to Sooltanpore, one comes across a few erect stones by the side of the road, and about twenty or thirty paces from these is to be found a small hut, with an enclosed courtyard. In front of the door-way to the hut is a Buddhist wheel, most clearly traced out on a flat stone in the ground, and on either side of the enclosure is a collection of erect stones, very much in form like those at Nuggur; but the figures on them are almost quite destroyed and untraceable. The people of the village have not the least idea where these sculpturings came from, or who put them into the field where they now lie.

# APPENDIX.

## STATISTICS OF DISTRICTS IN THE SUBDIVISION OF KOOLOO.

| Number. | NAMES. | Nono. | Negees. | Gyatpos. | Lumberdars. | Chowkeydars. | Rukhs.* | Area in Square Miles. | Revenue in Rupees. Khalsa.† | Maafee.‡ | | | Total. | | | Population. | Number of Begarees. |
|---|---|---|---|---|---|---|---|---|---|---|---|---|---|---|---|---|---|
| | | | | | | | | | Rupees. | R. | A. | P. | R. | A. | P. | | |
| 1 | 17 Kothees in Upper Beas Valley ......... | ... | 17 | ... | 64 | 23 | 25 | 674 | 27,459 | 12,345 | 8 | 0 | 39,804 | 8 | 0 | 33,410 | 5,167 |
| 2 | 6 Kothees in Wuzeeri-Rupi | ... | 6 | ... | 19 | 6 | 6 | 677 | ... | 10,931 | 2 | 9 | 10,931 | 2 | 9 | 12,496 | 1,197 |
| 3 | 25 Kothees in Seoraj ......... | ... | 26 | ... | 60 | 26 | 26 | 575 | 22,070 | 4,482 | 0 | 0 | 26,552 | 0 | 0 | 44,355 | 4,912 |
| 4 | 14 Kothees in Lahoul ...... | ... | 1 | ... | 14 | 14 | ... | 2,100 | 2,161 | 898 | 0 | 0 | 3,059 | 0 | 0 | 6,265 | 1,087 |
| 5 | 5 Kothees in Spiti ......... | 1 | ... | 5 | 5 | ... | ... | 2,199 | 753 | 37 | 4 | 0 | 790 | 4 | 0 | 2,272 | All the males and females do begar. |
| | | 1 | 50 | 5 | 162 | 65 | 57 | 6,025 | 52,443 | 28,693 | 14 | 9 | 81,136 | 14 | 9 | 98,798 | |

* Forest enclosures.

† Lands paying government revenue.

‡ Rent-free lands. The sums under this heading represent the actual values of the assessments, which, however, are never collected.

STATISTICS OF POPULATION, AREA, AND REVENUE PAYABLE IN THE SUBDIVISION OF KOOLOO FOR THE YEAR 1867 (THE CENSUS YEAR).

| DISTRICT. | Population. | Area in Square Miles. | Area in Acres. | MALGOOZAREE or ASSESSED LANDS. | | MINHAE or UNASSESSED LANDS. | | Demand on Account of Land Revenue for 1866–7 in Rupees. | Rate per Acre on Total Area. | | | Rate per Acre on Total Malgoozarie. | | | Rate per Acre on Total Cultivation. | | |
|---|---|---|---|---|---|---|---|---|---|---|---|---|---|---|---|---|---|
| | | | | Cultivated Acres. | Culturable Acres. | Lakhiraj Acres. | Barren Acres. | | R. | A. | P. | R. | A. | P. | R. | A. | P. |
| Kooloo | 98,798 | 6,025 | 3,984,500 | 27,515 | 6,632 | 783,618 | 3,166,735 | 52,443 | ... | ... | 4 | 1 | 14 | 11 | 1 | 15 | 9½ |

## STATISTICS OF THE RICE, OPIUM, AND TOBACCO CROPS IN KOOLOO.

| CROP. | Sowing Time. | Harvest. | Quantity of Seed per Acre for Planting out. | Produce per Acre. | Prices. | Where Sold. | REMARKS. |
|---|---|---|---|---|---|---|---|
| Rice ... | May. Seed germinates in 15 days, and is then transplanted. | September and October. | 42 to 46 seers. | 14 to 22 maunds.* | Rs. 2, Rs. 2 4, and Rs. 2 5 per maund. | To Lahoulees. | One maund of Dhan, well cleaned of the husk, leaves from 20 to 22 seers of (chawal) rice. |
| Opium .. | November. Seeds called "Post." | End of May. | 3 seers. | 6 maunds of seed and 10 seers of oil per maund. 7 to 8 seers of opium per acre. | Rs. 6 to Rs. 15 per pukha seer. | Kooloo, Mundee, and Bunneahs from the plains. | Red-blossomed poppy gives more opium and less seed than the white, and but little oil is obtained from the seed. The white poppy gives the best seed, and yields much oil. |
| Tobacco | April–May on irrigated land; June on unirrigated land. | August and September. | 3½ seers. | 10 to 12 maunds. | 6 to 8 seers per rupee. | Kooloo, Seoraj and Mundee. | |

* The maund is 40 seers, or 80 lb. English.

## GENEALOGICAL ROLL OF CHIEFS IN KOOLOO.

| No. | Name of Chief. | Remarks. |
|---|---|---|
| 1 | Behungamunnee | |
| 2 | Puch Pal | |
| 3 | Baheg Pal | |
| 4 | Doorheen Pal | |
| 5 | Soorg Pal | |
| 6 | Sooktee Pal | |
| 7 | Mahida Pal | |
| 8 | Oom Pal | |
| 9 | Rajinda Pal | |
| 10 | Busud Pal | |
| 11 | Busuda Pal | |
| 12 | Ootum Pal | The capital transferred from Juggutsookh to Nuggur. |
| 13 | Doja Pal | |
| 14 | Chukkur Pal | |
| 15 | Kurun Pal | |
| 16 | Sooruj Pal | |
| 17 | Ruxsh Pal | |
| 18 | Roodur Pal | |
| 19 | Haemur Pal | |
| 20 | Pursidh Pal | |
| 21 | Hurree Chund Pal | |
| 22 | Soobut Pal | |
| 23 | Saom Pal | |
| 24 | Sunsar Pal | |
| 25 | Bagh Pal | |
| 26 | Bubyah Pal | |
| 27 | Brahmo Pal | This Pal left no legitimate sons, and the chronicle says the Rajahs of Chumba, Ladakh, Sookhet, Bussahir, Kangra, |

GENEALOGICAL ROLL OF CHIEFS (*continued*).

| No. | Name of Chief. | Remarks. |
|---|---|---|
| | | and Bunghal made Gunaesh Pal his heir. |
| 28 | Gunaesh Pal | |
| 29 | Gumbheer Pal | |
| 30 | Bhoomee Pal | |
| 31 | Shureedut Taeshur Pal | In this reign there was war with Chumba, and Shureedut was killed by Umr Sing, Rajah of Chumba. Goburdun, it is said, reigned at this time at Indraput, *i.e.* Delhi. |
| 32 | Umr Pal | This chief fought with Chumba, and was slain with all his sons, except Seetul. |
| 33 | Seetul Pal | |
| 34 | Shirree Jerashur Pal | Aided by Bussahir troops, this chief expelled Chumba from Kooloo. As Seetul Pal was an exile, and does not appear to have ever reigned, as did not five of his descendants, it would seem that Kooloo must have been for some time anterior to Shirree Jerashur's reign, under the sway of Chumba. |
| 35 | Purkash Pal | |
| 36 | Ajumba Pal | |
| 37 | Tupanaeshur Pal | |
| 38 | Purum Pal | |
| 39 | Najindur Pal | |

GENEALOGICAL ROLL OF CHIEFS (*continued*).

| No. | Name of Chief. | Remarks. |
|---|---|---|
| 40 | Nard Pal | In this reign there was war with Chumba, and the Chumba troops advanced to Majna Kot, a village near the Rohtung pass, and there the Chumba Rajah built a fort. The strife continued for twelve years, when a peace was patched up, and the Kooloo people invited the Chumba soldiers to a feast, which was to be held at night. The men of Chumba were treacherously inveigled down to the banks of the Beas, where, falling over the steep precipices near Ralla, they were almost entirely destroyed. |
| 41 | Narotum Pal | |
| 42 | Shaesh Pal | |
| 43 | Bhoob Pal | |
| 44 | Janeerood Pal | |
| 45 | Hust Pal | |
| 46 | Soortee Pal | |
| 47 | Suntokh Pal | |
| 48 | Taegya Pal | |
| 49 | Oocht, or Kuchet Pal | |
| 50 | Sichundur Pal | It is stated this chief wen to the Delhi Rajah, complaining that the men of China had invaded his kingdom, and |

GENEALOGICAL ROLL OF CHIEFS (*continued*).

| No. | Name of Chief. | Remarks. |
| --- | --- | --- |
| | | that the Delhi Rajah himself headed an army, which marched through Kooloo, and took Gyamurr Orr (?) and Baltistan, with all the country as far as Mantilae (Manasorowa) Lake. |
| 51 | Surus Pal | |
| 52 | Saedaeb Pal | |
| 53 | Siri Mahadaeb Pal | |
| 54 | Nirtee Pal | In this reign Ali Shere Khan is said to have reigned in Cashmere. |
| 55 | Baen Pal | |
| 56 | Hust Pal | |
| 57 | Saesee Pal | |
| 58 | Gumbheer Pal | |
| 59 | Nisodhun Pal | |
| 60 | Narinda Pal | |
| 61 | Suntokh Pal | |
| 62 | Nundh Pal | |
| 63 | Dhurtee Pal | |
| 64 | Indur Pal | |
| 65 | Mahee Chukur Pal | |
| 66 | Yeodhur Pal | |
| 67 | Keral Pal | |
| 68 | Huns Pal | |
| 69 | Augusth Pal | |
| 70 | Muddun Pal | |
| 71 | Muddho Pal | |
| 72 | Oodhun Pal | |
| 73 | Kelas Pal | |

## GENEALOGICAL ROLL OF CHIEFS (*continued*).

| No. | Name of Chief. | Remarks. |
|---|---|---|
| 74 | Sidh Pal | This chief took the title of Sidh Sing. |
| 75 | Bahadur Sing | The kingdom of Kooloo was in this chief's reign consolidated, and very much enlarged. |
| 76 | Pertab Sing | |
| 77 | Purbut Sing | |
| 78 | Prithi Sing | |
| 79 | Kalian Sing | |
| 80 | Juggut Sing | Juggut Sing is said to have reigned sixty-one years. He was a powerful sovereign, who considerably extended his dominions by conquest. He had the image of Rognath-Ji brought up from Oudh, and introduced the worship of Vishnoo into Kooloo. He lived during the latter part of the reign of Shah Jehan and the earlier years of Aurungzib's rule. Sooltanpore was made the capital. |
| 81 | Boodh Sing | In Boodh Sing's reign the kingdom of Kooloo became a really important state. All Kooloo, Wuzeeri-Rupi, Seoraj, Lahoul, Spiti, Bussahir, Bunghal, a great portion of Mundee and Sookhet, with the hill |

GENEALOGICAL ROLL OF CHIEFS (*continued*).

| No. | Name of Chief. | Remarks. |
|---|---|---|
| | | states close up to Simla, were under this chief's sway. |
| 82 | Maun Sing | Maun Sing entirely subdued Mundee, but again gave up the country. |
| 83 | Raj Sing | |
| 84 | Jae Sing | Jae Sing went to Lahore to ask for aid against Mundee. |
| 85 | Tedhi Sing | |
| 86 | Prithum Sing | The country in this reign was torn by internal dissensions. |
| 87 | Brikhama Sing | In this reign the Sikhs invaded Kooloo; this was about 1812. |
| 88 | Jeet Sing | The last reigning chief of Kooloo. He was deposed by the Sikhs in 1840. |
| | Thakoor Sing | Thakoor Sing was granted the title of Rajah by Maha-Rajah Shere Sing, and made Jaghirdar of Wuzeeri-Rupi. |
| | Gyan Sing | There were some doubts as to Gyan Sing's legitimacy, and while confirming him in the jaghirdarship his father held, the British Government only granted him the title of Rae. |
| | Dhuleep Sing | Dhuleep Sing is a minor. He is under the tuition of Pundit Nathoo Ram, and promises to turn out well. |

## PORTERAGE HIRE AT VARIOUS STAGES IN KOOLOO, LAHOUL, AND SPITI.

| No. | FROM | TO | Annas. |
|---|---|---|---|
| 1 | Sooltanpore......... | Raesun ............ | 3 |
| 2 | ,, ......... | Dobee ............... | 3 |
| 3 | ,, ......... | Nuggur ............ | 4 |
| 4 | ,, ......... | Bajoura ............ | 3 |
| 5 | ,, ......... | Bijli Mahdeo ...... | 3 |
| 6 | ,, ......... | Chawān ............ | 4 |
| 7 | ,, ......... | Kuronw ............ | 3 |
| 8 | ,, ......... | Buin.................. | 3 |
| 9 | Raesun or Dobee... | Rampore ............ | 3 |
| 10 | Raesum ........... | Nuggur ............ | 3 |
| 11 | ,, ........... | Menalee (double march)......... | 6 |
| 12 | Dobee .............. | Nuggur ............ | 2 |
| 13 | ,, by right bank of Beas ......... | Menalee ............ | 4 |
| | ,, left ,, | Juggutsookh ...... | 4 |
| 14 | Nuggur ........... | Juggutsookh ...... | 3 |
| 15 | ,, ........... | Jijmole ............ | 2 |
| | ,, ........... | Menalee ............ | 4 |
| 16 | Juggutsookh ...... | Menalee ............ | 2 |
| 17 | ,, ......... | Basisht............... | 3 |
| 18 | ,, ......... | Chikkun ............ | 4 |
| 19 | ,, ......... | Pulchan ............ | 3 |
| 20 | Menalee ........... | Basisht.............. | 2 |
| 21 | ,, ........... | Pulchan ............ | 2 |
| 22 | ,, ........... | Ralla ............... | 3 |
| 23 | ,, ........... | Rampore ............ | 3 |
| 24 | Pulchan ........... | Ralla ............... | 3 |

PORTERAGE HIRE, &c. (*continued*).

| No. | FROM | TO | Annas. |
|---|---|---|---|
| 25 | Pulchan ........... | Koksur ........... | 9 |
| 26 | " ........... | Up Solung valley per march ... | 2 |
| 27 | " ........... | To end of Solung valley ........ | 3 |
| 28 | Ralla .............. | Koksur ........... | 6 |
| 29 | Koksur ........... | Sissoo .............. | 4 |
| 30 | Sissoo .............. | Gondla.............. | 3 |
| 31 | Gondla.............. | Kielung ........... | 3 |
| 32 | Kielung ........... | Kolung ........... | 4 |
| 33 | Kolung ........... | Darcha.............. | 3 |
| 34 | Darcha.............. | Putseo .............. | 3 |
| 35 | Putseo .............. | Zingzingbar......... | 3 |
| 36 | Zingzingbar......... | Kenlang ........... | 6 |
| 37 | Kenlang ........... | Tserap river ...... | 4 |
| 38 | Zingzingbar......... | Togpo Goma ...... | 6 |
| 39 | Togpo Goma ...... | Togpo Yukma...... | 4 |
| 40 | Togpo Yukma...... | Chundra Dull ...... | 4 |
| 41 | Chundra Dull ...... | Sittee Kar ......... | 4 |
| 42 | Kuronw ........... | Budwanee ......... | 4 |
| 43 | Chawan ........... | Jhirree.............. | 3 |
| 44 | Jhirree.............. | Manikurn ......... | 3 |
| 45 | Manikurn ......... | Rusole .............. | 3 |
| 46 | Rusole .............. | Malauna ........... | 4 |
| 47 | Malauna ........... | Jijmole ........... | 4 |
| 48 | Chikkun ........... | Chaitroo ........... | 4 |
| 49 | Chaitroo ........... | Futteh Roonee ... | 4 |
| 50 | Futteh Roonee ... | Karcha ........... | 4 |
| 51 | Karcha ........... | Losur .............. | 4 |
| 52 | Losur .............. | Khiotto ........... | 4 |

## PORTERAGE HIRE, &c. (*continued*).

| No. | FROM | TO | Annas. |
|---|---|---|---|
| 53 | Khiotto ............ | Khiebur ............ | 4 |
| 54 | Khiebur ............ | Kazeh ............... | 4 |
| 55 | Kazeh ............... | Dhunkur ............ | 4 |
| 56 | Losur ............... | Sittee Kar ......... | 3 |
| | **SIMLA STAGES.** | | |
| 57 | Sooltanpore ......... | Bajoura ............ | 3 |
| | Bajoura ............ | Dulasnee ............ | 2 |
| 58 | " ............ | Larjee ............... | 4 |
| 59 | " ............ | Kamand ............ | 4 |
| | Dulasnee ............ | Larjee ............... | 2 |
| 60 | Larjee ............... | Munglor ............ | 3 |
| 61 | " ............... | Plach ............... | 4 |
| 62 | Munglor ............ | Jebee ............... | 3 |
| 63 | Jebee ............... | Kot .................. | 4 |
| 64 | Kot .................. | Chawai............... | 3 |
| 65 | Chawai............... | Dalash ............... | 3 |
| 66 | Dalash ............... | Kotghur or Kom- harsen ......... | 4 |

ALFRED HARCOURT,

*Assistant-Commissioner of Kooloo.*

24*th May*, 1870.

## A SHORT VOCABULARY OF MALAUNA WORDS.

| English. | Oordoo. | Malauna. |
|---|---|---|
| One | Aek | Id, Eed |
| Two | Do | Nish |
| Three | Tin | Shum |
| Four | Char | Pooh |
| Five | Panch | Nahan |
| Twenty | Bis | Beeh Nabya |
| One Hundred | Aek Sau | Nabeeha |
| Wheat | Gundum | Jhand |
| Barley | Jow | Chahg |
| Black Mustard | Sarson | Shaee |
| Rice | Chawul | Lar |
| Purified Butter | Ghee | Mar |
| Milk | Dudh | Kheerang |
| Butter | Mukhun | Boohur |
| Honey | Shahad | Was |
| Salt | Nimuk | Chah |
| Bread | Rotee | Horá |
| Loose Trousers | Paijamas | Soothana |
| Clothes | Kapra | Gasa |
| Cow | Gae | Hooch |
| Ox | Bail | Rahad |
| Young Bull | Bachha | Shakras |
| Young Cow | Bachchee | Shakreech |
| Sheep | Bher | Khas |
| Wool | Oon | Chám |
| Necklace | Kanthee | Kortheega |
| Mother | Máñ | Ya |
| Father | Bap | Bá |
| Son | Beta | Chhah |

## A SHORT VOCABULARY, &c. (*continued*).

| ENGLISH. | OORDOO. | MALAUNA. |
|---|---|---|
| Daughter | Betee | Cheemee |
| Fire-wood | Balan | Shing |
| Water | Pani | Tee |
| Rain | Barish | Jab |
| Ice | Baraf | Chous |
| Stone | Patthr | Pan |
| Grass | Ghas | Cheeh |
| Field | Khet | Sah |
| Wife | Aurut | Chhes |
| Thou | Tu | Ka |
| I | Main | Goo |
| Fat | Mota | Polak |
| Thin | Putla | Julach |
| Hollow | Palla | Palung |
| Strong | Muzbut | Jorkaras |
| Hair | Bal | Karah |
| Ear | Kan | Raoo or Rad |
| Cheek | Galh | Peeng |
| Nose | Nak | Tanh |
| Mouth | Munh | Khukang |
| Tongue | Jibh | Lae |
| Tooth | Daut | Gar |
| Eye | Ankh | Meega |
| Neck | Gurdun | Moothung |
| Breast | Chhatee | Shahan |
| Foot | Pawn | Thurla |
| Hand | Hath | Talang |
| Finger | Angootha | Parad |
| Mine | Mera | Aka |
| Yours | Tera | Kanka |
| Morning | Soobah | Soham |

## A SHORT VOCABULARY, &c. (*continued*).

| ENGLISH. | OORDOO. | MALAUNA. |
|---|---|---|
| Evening | Sham | Uberang |
| Darkness | Andhera | Niharas |
| Day | Din | Dhyaree |
| Clouds | Badul | Joosangee |
| Rainy Season | Bursat | Saul |
| Year | Sal | Teeleeng |
| Forest | Ban, Jungle | Reeyas |
| Cold | Thanda | Liskee |
| Fire | Ag | Meeh |
| Earth | Zamin | Dhurt |
| Man | Admi | Marsang |
| Yes | Han | Hoe |
| No or Not | Nahin | Maee |
| Beneath | Niche | Yen |
| White | Sufed | Chhog |
| Dirty | Maila | Juheh |
| Black | Kala | Bok |
| Dog | Kutta | Koee |
| Cat | Bullee | Booraree |
| Bear | Bhalu | Hom |

THE END.

WYMAN AND SONS, PRINTERS, GREAT QUEEN STREET, LONDON, W.C.

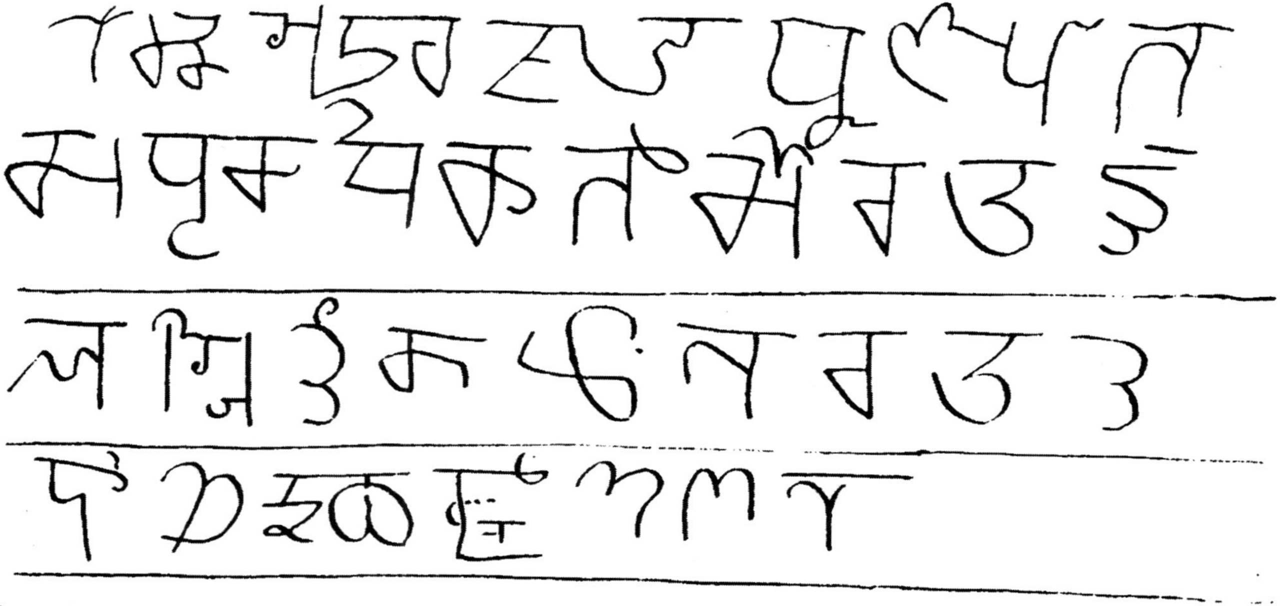

Inscriptions on the left side of thc entrance to the Jugutsookh Pent-roofed Temple. The three first lines follow each other in the order here given, and the last is by itself on the front face.